I Blew Up My Life, and I've Never Been HAPPIER

D1209024

Amber James

Copyright © 2023 by Amber James.
All rights reserved.

No part of this publication may be reproduced, scanned, or distributed in any form without written permission from the author. For permission requests, email contact@notestoselfshop.com.

Disclaimer: The information provided in this book is for educational, informational, and entertainment purposes only. Neither the publisher nor the author is engaged in rendering professional advice or services to the reader. The ideas and suggestions provided in this book are not intended as a substitute for seeking professional guidance. Neither the publisher nor the author shall be held liable or responsible for any loss or damage allegedly arising from any suggestion or information contained in this book.

The events and conversations in this book have been recorded to the best of the author's ability, although some names and details have been changed to protect the privacy of individuals.

ISBN 979-8-9870149-1-2
Cover Photography © Heather Tabacchi
First Edition 2023

DEDICATION

To Mom and Dad –

Thanks for letting me pursue my wildest dreams.
I love you.

"You only live once, but if you do it right, once is enough."

– Mae West

AUTHOR'S NOTE

The title of this book is no exaggeration. I did, indeed, blow up my life—in the most epic and liberating way possible. As you dive into the pages of *I Blew Up My Life, and I've Never Been Happier*, you are about to embark on a raw, unfiltered journey with me.

The vulnerability required to bare my soul and reveal my darkest moments was overwhelming, but I knew I had to share my story in hopes of helping others. When I hit my rock bottom, I yearned for stories from other women who took a chance on themselves and found happiness on the other side. In this longing, I realized the power of shared experiences and their profound impact on our lives; that is why you're holding this book now.

This book isn't just about my journey, though; it's about the potential for change that is within all of us. It's a reminder that no matter where you are in life or how stuck or unfulfilled you might feel, you always have the power to forge a new path.

If you're debating leaving a toxic job or relationship, dealing with the unbearable heaviness of grief, facing intimidating health challenges, or searching for a rainbow amid a storm —this book is my hand reaching out to you as a friend who has been there.

I'm here to tell you that on the other side of the explosion, a life that is authentically yours, filled with happiness and purpose, is waiting for you.

You possess the strength to walk away from anything (or anyone) that doesn't bring you joy and toward a life that resonates with your wildest dreams.

As you read this book, please ask yourself: What is your current life costing you? Is it your health, freedom, sanity, peace, happiness, time, or all of the above? Would you encourage a best friend to stay in the circumstances you've been settling for?

The following essays and recollections described in this book happened to me and have been reconstructed based on conversations with family and friends, journal entries, and my memory. Names and identifying characteristics of people described in my book have been changed to protect their privacy, but all the stories are true.

Please note this book explores and contains content that may be unsettling to some readers, including references to alcohol consumption, emotional abuse, and suicidal thoughts.

I am not an expert, a therapist, or a trained professional, so if you or someone you know is struggling, don't be afraid to seek help, and please take care of yourself while reading.

The vulnerable stories within this book are shared with the hope that they will resonate, heal, and inspire—a truth

I've come to appreciate as a journalist. My entire life, I have lived by the saying, "Everyone has a story," and now it's time to tell mine.

CONTENTS

PART THREE
RISING FROM THE ASHES

INTRODUCTION

Growing up, I did everything by the book. I studied hard in school, didn't touch any drugs, and went to church every Sunday. Every decision was carefully choreographed to maintain harmony, meet expectations, and make everyone around me happy. It wasn't that I was a conformist by nature; I didn't know any better.

From a young age, I understood my role: the good girl, the obedient daughter, and the diligent student. My brother, on the other hand, was the quintessential rebel who dared to question and defy expectations. Caught in the duality of our roles, I clung even tighter to the straight and narrow path, shouldering the responsibility of being the steady and predictable one. No one explicitly instructed me to act this way, but somewhere along the way, I took it upon myself to step into this role.

The expectations of others became my compass. Their happiness was my north star. I became an expert in not rocking the boat and maintaining the delicate balance that seemed to hold my universe together.

On the surface, I focused on looking good on the outside and checking the boxes, hoping to exceed everyone's expectations of me. But beneath this carefully constructed exterior, I struggled to find my place. The more I tried to fit in and reach perfection, the more I felt like a stranger to myself. Growing up in rural Ohio, the cross of Christianity cast a long shadow over my life. In this bubble of faith, I naively assumed that the entire world was a mirror of our little community, bound by the same beliefs. I believed my actions, however small, could be the deciding factor for my eternal fate. Heaven or Hell—these two monumental destinies seemed to hinge upon my every choice, and the enormity of this fiery, eternal punishment loomed over me. Despite the absurdity of a child bearing such a burden, I swallowed my doubts. To question anything was like a dance with the Devil that I dared not entertain.

But that didn't stop my brain from overanalyzing every little detail. During the sermons and Sunday school lessons, my mind filled with questions that seemed to unravel my entire religious upbringing, like could I have the same fate as the Virgin Mary and conceive a child, even if I didn't have sex? Such a thought sent shivers of uncertainty and fear down my spine.

I also wondered how God, the embodiment of love and compassion, could harbor such disdain towards homosexuality. The contradiction was striking, and my young heart failed to reconcile this disparity. Up to this point, I'd only met one openly gay man. He had an undeniable zest for life and was caring and non-judgemental. How could a loving God send this man to Hell?! I tried to suppress these thoughts believing this internal voice was the Devil trying to "trick" me. So I didn't dare speak up. I saw what happened to those who challenged the Bible's teachings and didn't want to face those consequences. One took physical shape in the "black snake," a black leather whip used to maintain discipline and control. I never saw it used, but the very mention of it was enough to elicit silence, serving as a deterrent against disobedience.

I pushed down my need for answers. But with that, I found myself doubting my very existence. The voice was relentless, amplifying my thoughts and growing louder by the day. *Was this the only script I could follow? Was this all there was to life?* Deep down, a quiet rebellion began to stir within me.

In the solitude of my bedroom, I began to dream of a different life where I could choose my destiny. I wished for a place where I could belong, not because I fit a predetermined mold, but because I was myself, flaws and all. I found peace and adventure in the realms of my imagination.

With a pen and a blank page, I dreamt up vibrant stories that would whisk me away to distant lands and mystical places. These narratives were my escape, my secret passageway to the vast universe beyond the confines of my small town.

In the stories, I explored enchanted forests and navigated through bustling cities. I was not the "good girl"; I was an adventurer, heroine, and dreamer who lived life on her terms. Through these tales, I lived a thousand lives, each one thrilling and liberating, offering me a glimpse of the 'more' I desperately wanted.

My hometown provided a wholesome upbringing, but there was a persistent sense that I didn't belong and that a bigger life was out there. At that time, I didn't quite understand what that meant for me, so I focused on what I could control: my grades, my accolades, and pretty much anything that would set me free to find my place in this big, wild world. It was a commitment to myself, a silent pact I would hold on to until I could step into the world on my own.

Two days before my eighteenth birthday, I received the best gift of all: I got accepted into my dream school, E.W. Scripps School of Journalism, at Ohio University. I had always wanted to be a writer, and this was the next step to get me there. At the time, the journalism program was ranked one of the best in the country.

The college town in Athens, Ohio, was a two-hour car ride from my home but seemed like an entirely different universe. The small-town bubble encapsulating my first 18 years burst open, ushering in a refreshing, exhilarating breath of new experiences.

I shared a cramped dorm room with a stranger and took the top bunk, even though I secretly feared rolling off in the middle of the night. Our lifestyles were so different; she was the life of the party, going out every night while I struggled with my new-found freedom and shedding my "good girl" image. In an attempt to be cool around my new roommate and her friends, I took my first sip of alcohol - a Natural Light - and smoked pot. I was such an amateur.

"Mmm," I murmured as the watery, metallic taste of the beer went down my throat. Then came the joint; I inhaled quickly, resulting in a prolonged coughing fit—rookie mistake.

But soon, I found my people: a dedicated group of aspiring journalists who worked at the student-run newspaper. *The Post* newsroom was far from glamorous, but it was a place that pulsed with life and purpose. It had real character. There was a damp, inexplicable whiff of sewer that stubbornly clung to the walls, and the floor was a mosaic of unidentifiable stains.

Despite its physical shortcomings, the newsroom was a creative space where I was a part of something bigger than myself. When I hunched over the keyboard of a Bondi blue iMac amidst other like-minded writers, this unlikely space and these people became home. (These friendships, forged by late-night deadlines and shared ambitions, have mostly stood the test of time. Many of my friends now work at prestigious publications like *The New York Times*, *The Washington Post*, and *Baltimore Sun*.)

As I began to carve out a niche for myself on the culture staff at *The Post*, my life took on a rhythm of its own. I was conversing with fascinating individuals, from iconic figures like Nancy Cartwright, the long-time voice of Bart Simpson on the animated television series *The Simpsons*, to passionate musicians of local college bands. Each story was a step away from my small-town upbringing and toward realizing my dreams. My peers and professors taught me to ask probing questions and not accept things at face value. It also led me to dig deeper and question everything, especially in a world riddled with misinformation. I even began to rethink everything I had once accepted without hesitation. The strict doctrines and beliefs that had once formed the bedrock of my existence now seemed absurd. I gradually distanced myself from the church and embarked on a spiritual journey that didn't involve a divine entity wielding power with an iron fist.

Within the newsroom's soundtrack of clattering keyboards, the laughter of inside jokes, and a noisy police scanner, I found a community vastly different from the one I had grown up in. It was a space where diversity, curiosity, and authenticity were welcomed and celebrated.

As my college graduation approached, I was not the same person who had entered that tiny dorm room four years prior. I was ready to take on the world, armed with a degree and an unwavering belief in the power of journalism. I had stories to tell, and I was ready to embark on a career that would allow me to do just that.

However, despite applying to numerous newspaper and magazine opportunities, I found myself without a job offer. It felt like a sucker punch, especially considering the successful trajectories of my peers. I thought maybe this was God's way of punishing me for distancing myself from the church and not going to a Bible college to get an "MRS Degree." (For those who aren't familiar, MRS degree is a slang term used to describe a woman who pursues a college education to find a spouse.) The complex emotions of shame and guilt stirred a storm within, challenging the peace I sought in my journey of self-discovery.

I was driven by a deep-seated need to validate my decisions and demonstrate to everyone around me - and perhaps, more importantly, to myself - that the choices I made were indeed the right ones. So, I forcefully pushed these unsettling sentiments to the recesses of my mind and kept moving forward.

Note to Self:
Take a chance
on yourself and
never give up.

Armed with determination and a naive willingness to take risks even during The Great Recession, I packed my life into two suitcases and moved to New York City.

To me, the Big Apple was a world of possibilities where I believed I could make my mark. The iconic melody of Frank Sinatra's "New York, New York" echoed in my mind as I looked to my future. His love letter to the city was more than just a tune, but an anthem of hope and aspiration propelling me forward. New York City, with its towering skyscrapers and pulsating energy, was the stage upon which I intended to prove myself.

Thankfully, my gamble paid off. Within two weeks of moving to the city, I got hired to cover entertainment news and interview Hollywood's biggest stars. The lives of Jennifer Aniston, Brad Pitt, and Betty White (R.I.P.) were part of my daily conversations. Colleagues and I would discuss the latest gossip about these stars (instead of the weather) and dissect every detail as if these stars were our close friends. At one point, I even found myself well-versed in the world of the Kardashians and Jenners, knowing every name, age, star sign, and significant other of these reality stars, as if they were part of my extended family. I was in deep.

My days were filled with concerts and exclusive parties. I often wondered, *How did I get so lucky?* It was thrilling, intoxicating even, and I reveled in the glitz and glamour of it all ... until the luster began to fade.

There were days when celebrities, primarily men, treated me with little regard, degrading my worth to mere insignificance. I was brought back to that scared little girl, nervous about rocking the boat or speaking up because these men were too powerful. I let them yell at me, believing I did something wrong or it was my fault. Then, a voice cut through my introspection. *Anyone would kill to be a red carpet reporter. You should be grateful! This is just part of the job. Suck it up.* The words rang in my ears, shattering the silence. It was a brutal reminder of the ruthlessness of the entertainment industry. But the weight of these volatile interactions caught up with me when I was alone. I spent many tear-filled nights sprawled out on the cool ceramic tiles of my bathroom floor with a bottle of Cabernet Sauvignon beside me. The choices I had made in my career, once worn as badges of accomplishment, suddenly bore down on me like a burden. Was the ladder I had been climbing worth it?

Despite what happened behind closed doors, I showcased my stunning and fabulous career in public and social media - only showing the highlights. I powered through those painful interactions... for a while. But when directives from superiors involved me tailing celebrities to the bathroom or loitering around their houses in upstate New York, I questioned the integrity of my work. The relentless pressure to find salacious stories and unearth a scandal drained me. It starkly contrasted what initially drew me to this career ten years earlier. I was in the business of storytelling, not tearing people down. It wasn't long before I was ousted.

Although I was devastated to lose my job, it was a blessing in disguise. Still, there was a chip on my shoulder. I spiraled into a web of imposter syndrome and wondered when I'd ever be "good enough."

Over the next few years, I landed other jobs. Some good. Some bad. But I was in a constant race, ceaselessly hustling, always chasing the next milestone, hoping it would finally bring me happiness and the external validation I desperately wanted. But even after negotiating a hundred-thousand-dollar branded content deal, dabbling in real estate, and working at one of the largest media companies, I still was unfulfilled. I was in a neverending pursuit for validation, and the hardest person to please was myself. The hunger for growth and accomplishment was insatiable, though, so I continued to hustle.

I convinced myself that answering work emails at midnight and being blunt, anxious, and stressed were part of being a *real* New Yorker. I complained about my subway commute, the increasing rents, and the dizzying stimulation with pride. I began normalizing the hustle culture as a symbol of my success.

By my mid-30s, I had accomplished everything society told me I needed to be successful and happy.

- ✓ I was dating a successful guy.
- ✓ I lived in a beautiful apartment in Manhattan.
- ✓ I traveled the world.
- ✓ I had a six-figure salary.
- ✓ I was in the best shape of my life.

By all accounts, I should have been happy, but my insides told a different story. The illusion of stability offered by corporate America actually left me hollow. No matter what I attained, I grappled with feelings of not being good enough, intelligent enough, "wifey" enough, loveable enough, or thin enough.

Note to Self:
What you tell
yourself can
build you up or
tear you down.
#SelfTalkMatters

I fantasized about leaving my New York life behind and heading on a new adventure, but the unknown was terrifying, so I stayed in my comfort zone, running toward a goal post that kept moving.

Deep down, I hoped to go all-in on my dreams—one day. I wanted to become a full-time author, start a business, and share my stories with the world. Still, that later date kept getting pushed back farther and farther. Without an actual deadline, though, I stuck to the status quo and kept grinding. I tried to reconcile that perhaps I was disillusioned; maybe my expectations about success were all wrong.

Life is funny, though. As soon I leaned into my "comfortable" existence, the global COVID-19 pandemic dealt a crushing blow to my perceived stability. The city that never sleeps became a ghost town overnight, and my years of hustling came to a grinding halt.

Now stripped of my daily commutes and the numbness brought by happy hour libations, I was forced to slow down and look inward. I could no longer divert my attention away from the sense of inadequacy that continually shadowed my accomplishments. This unpredictable time took me on a wild journey—full of love, loss, grief, discovery, and heartbreak —forcing me to reevaluate every aspect of my life. I soon learned that sometimes everything has to blow up to make room for a world of possibilities, freedom, and, most importantly, happiness.

This is my story.

PART ONE

Ticking Time Bomb

CHAPTER ONE

The Good, The Bad, and The Tiger King

"All future conferences and travel are on hold - indefinitely," the CEO stated during a late-February 2020 call with leaders.

The open floor plan made it impossible not to overhear conversations, even when you weren't intentionally eavesdropping. But I was definitely tuning into this one.

Whispers about the COVID-19 virus had steadily escalated for months, and now it was creeping closer and closer to New York City. I attempted to keep my anxieties in check, but it was getting more difficult by the day. My brain could not fathom a world where travel was non-existent, and seclusion and masks would be just another part of life. It was Sci-fi, shit. Not my life. Not right now.

"Where does this leave us?" I asked my coworker Colin, rolling my chair over to his desk.

He shrugged. "I have no idea."

And so, we returned to the tasks at hand.

By mid-afternoon, our inboxes chimed with a company-wide email announcing that we'd be transitioning to remote work until further notice. I remember feeling a wave of naive optimism, assuming my coworkers and I would return to the office after a few weeks.

"See you soon," I told my boss, placing my laptop, chargers, and stack of notebooks into my bag.

I left my workspace in slight disarray. I abandoned framed photos of my family, thank-you notes from clients, and the New York City Police Foundation's 2020 Canine & Friends calendar, featuring NYPD's four-legged partners (dogs and horses) in action. I had no idea the world would turn upside down or that the next two years would challenge my strength, resilience, and values.

* * *

"The World Health Organization has officially declared the novel coronavirus outbreak a global pandemic," a news reporter stated on the television screen.

New York City became the grim epicenter of America's coronavirus crisis. Once filled with friends and laughter, the outside world now felt like a battlefield where anyone and everyone might be an unwitting foe. We were all living in a horror movie. Nurses and doctors bore the scars of this relentless battle. The masks they clung to as their only shield had become a precious commodity, held under lock and key. Outside these hospitals, bodies of coronavirus victims piled up in refrigerated trailers, converted into makeshift morgues.

During this unprecedented time, I was sequestered within the confines of an 800-square-foot apartment with my boyfriend, Luke. We moved into this beautiful apartment two weeks before the city shut down and still had boxes to unpack. Our dreams of hosting lively dinner parties on our balcony, which offered enchanting views of the Statue of Liberty, were abruptly put on hold.

The initial excitement of working from home dwindled rapidly when the boundaries between my professional and personal life started to blur. The confines of our apartment, which once felt spacious, now seemed to shrink with every passing day. My makeup vanity in the bedroom turned into my remote workstation, while the dinner table and living room served as Luke's office, where he took calls all day.

My bedroom, which once provided solace and relaxation, now constantly reminded me of the job that was now intruding into my personal space. My sanctuary was compromised, and I felt the walls closing in.

At night, I wrapped myself up like a burrito in the sheets, trying to ignore the gravitational force which emanated from my laptop's sleek exterior. My work computer seemed to taunt me, reminding me of unfinished tasks, unanswered emails, and looming work deadlines. I toyed with the idea of relocating my laptop. But where could it go? The bathroom? New York apartments are infamous for their compact sizes. It was tolerable when the apartment merely served as a place to rest after a long day. But now, it was my entire world.

As the weeks passed, Luke and I camped out on the couch watching episodes of *Tiger King*. This trashy yet wildly captivating docuseries delved into the bizarre world and rivalry between two big cat owners, the flamboyant Joe Exotic and the enigmatic Carole Baskin. The show took our minds off the loss happening outside our apartment.

"Luke, how are we going to navigate this pandemic?" I asked.

He looked at me, his eyes soft with understanding, "I wish I had a clear answer."

"But we've got each other, right?" I asked, my voice barely a whisper.

"Always," he replied, grabbing my hand. "We're in this together, and that's how we'll get through it - together."

During this time of uncertainty, his words offered comfort and reassurance.

Our relationship wasn't perfect, but it was ours, and for the time being, it was enough.

By summer, I was living out a real-life version of Groundhog Day. Each morning, I'd stumble out of bed around 8:30 a.m., mechanically brush my teeth, throw my hair in a bun, whip up some coffee, and warily check the escalating numbers of the city's COVID-19 deaths. Then, I'd slide into a pair of yoga pants and a matching top, which somehow felt like a small victory amidst the monotony, and by 9 a.m., I was in work mode. The longer the pandemic lasted, the more I worked. It was as if my backside seemingly fused with the chair.

"It's like I've sprouted roots," I joked to Luke one evening, attempting to lighten the mood.

While the world around me seemed stuck in a monotonous loop, my body was charting its own course. The physical changes were evident. I had the unwelcome addition of extra pounds, and now silver strands glistened in my hair, weaving a tale of stress that I was living but not acknowledging. More alarming was the cocktail of mental strain that had accumulated over the months of the pandemic. Internally, I was a precarious time bomb, teetering on the brink of a catastrophic explosion.

In this challenging time, I didn't know how to show up for myself, let alone advocate for my needs. With countless people far worse off, it seemed indulgent to wallow in my despair.

Note to Self:
It's okay
to not
be okay.

I could not disconnect from the intensity of it all, and my anxiety only got worse when several colleagues, including Colin, were unceremoniously laid off via Zoom. It was a harsh wake-up call, reminding us that job security was never guaranteed.

"So, who will run our social media accounts now that Colin is gone?" I messaged my boss.

"Amber, do you have a moment to chat?" the reply pinged from my boss. This message added another layer of uncertainty to the situation.

"Would you be willing to oversee our accounts?" my boss asked me.

I took a moment, inhaling deeply. On the one hand, the proposition was a compliment and an opportunity for career advancement. But on the other hand, I was already struggling to manage my workload. I was curious to know how I could shoulder the responsibilities of a full-time social media manager.

Even though my mind was saying, "No, I do not want to do that," my mouth said, "Yes, no problem." As a people-pleaser, I did not want to disappoint people, especially my boss. I could not summon the bravery to reject these added duties, so I asked for more money. Advocating for my worth filled me with a sense of empowerment - for a few hours.

Regrettably, even though my boss championed my case, the company's counteroffer discouraged me. I wanted a raise that reflected the skills, experience, and contributions I had already made to the organization. Instead, the number on the table seemed underwhelming, considering the additional tasks I'd be taking on.

It was a challenging reminder that even when we, as women, stand up for ourselves and demand a rightful increase in our wages, it doesn't necessarily guarantee the desired outcome.

Those feelings led me back to a familiar place of guilt and shame. I was conditioned to think that I should be content and satisfied with what was offered. That's the narrative I had been taught all my life. However, this only fueled feelings of resentment within me.

My dissatisfaction was not about greed; it was about fairness. This realization was a tough pill to swallow, though, because I worked hard and poured my time and energy into the company, consistently delivering results. I knew I deserved more money.

Still, I begrudgingly accepted the offer and the new job responsibilities with one caveat. After thirty days, we'd reconvene to discuss compensation again.

Note to Self:
Get everything
in writing!

I tried to convince myself the offer was not a reflection of my worth as an individual; it was simply an outcome within the company's budget. I focused instead on what I could control: my actions, my mindset, and my ongoing professional development -- whether it was at my current company or, more than likely, seeking employment elsewhere.

Later that night over dinner, I opened up to Luke about my plight.

"The company did increase my salary," I started, glancing at him across the dinner table, "but it's nowhere near what I should be earning for this new role."

"Well, how much are we talking about?" his brows furrowed in confusion.

I hesitantly gave him the figure.

His reaction was immediate and visceral.

"That's all they could give you?" he questioned.

"I know, I know," I murmured.

Luke's expression hardened. "And, you actually accepted that amount of money?"

"What choice did I have, Luke? I didn't want to seem ungrateful or difficult. People are losing their jobs out there," I said.

"Amber, they're exploiting you," he said, shaking his head in disappointment.

A mixture of defeat and frustration raged through me. I felt like a failure to myself and now with Luke. I knew he was right, but it was easier said than done.

Despite my disappointment, I was determined to excel and prove my worth. I worked around the clock, seven days a week, pouring my heart into managing our social media accounts while maintaining my previous workload. Each crafted post and strategic campaign was a testament to my commitment and dedication to the company.

I hoped my efforts would clarify the company's priorities and where I fit into it. But my efforts remained largely unseen because we all worked remotely. There were no colleagues to witness my late-night work sessions and no boss to observe the meticulous attention to detail that went into every task.

My dedication was disappearing into the digital void, as was my enthusiasm. The disparity between my efforts and my compensation was growing.

Making matters worse, the follow-up meeting about compensation got postponed. Each delay felt like a slap in the face, eroding my confidence and trust in the company. The enthusiasm and drive that once defined my work ethic was replaced by resentment and burnout. I felt underappreciated, undervalued, and utterly drained. We're told that hard work is the secret to success, but hard work alone doesn't always pay off.

CHAPTER TWO

A Voyage Cut Short

Joy coursed through me as the distinctive ring of a FaceTime call echoed from my phone. My grandparents were reaching out to wish me a happy birthday. Their smiles filled my display as they launched into a duet, singing the birthday melody.

"Happy birthday to you,
Happy birthday to you,
Happy birthday, dear Amber Sue,
Happy birthday to you..."

Their voices, filled with such love, brought tears to my eyes. They continued with their signature twist on the song

- an inside joke that had become an important part of the tradition.

"...And many more on Channel 4,
And Scooby Doo on Channel 2."

This annual serenade was the only gift I needed.

It had been a while since I had seen my grandparents in person. I visited Ohio in early February to celebrate my grandpa's birthday. That weekend became a cherished gift of togetherness before the world went into lockdown.

"How's our New York City girl?" my grandpa asked.

"I'm even better now," I smiled, strolling along the boardwalk in Hoboken, New Jersey, taking in the breathtaking views of Manhattan. (This side of the Hudson River became my sanctuary, providing tranquility away from the city.)

"Grandpa," I said, "is this where the boys tried to steal your sailor hat when you were in the Navy?"

He let out a delighted chuckle. "You remember that?"

"Of course," I responded. "It's one of my favorite stories."

My grandpa was a gifted storyteller, sharing tales of his service in the 1950s while on the USS Des Moines. He repeatedly told me one particular story of when the ship docked in Hoboken.

"As a sailor, you always had to hold onto your hat," he'd say, "Otherwise, those kids would try to swipe it and run away."

I imagined that my grandfather was as mischievous as those young Hoboken boys when he was their age because, even in his 80s, he loved a good prank.

After sharing a few more laughs and catching up about our lives, it was time to say goodbye.

"I love you. Be good, and stay safe," my grandpa said, adding, "And tell Luke to take care of our girl."

"I will," I promised. "I love you too, and I'll call you soon."

That would be the last time I spoke to my grandfather. The last time I'd hear his laughter. The last time he'd tell me he loved me.

* * *

Thanksgiving arrived, but it bore a stark contrast to the festivities we enjoyed in previous years, filled with family, laughter, and the rich aroma of a home-cooked meal. Instead, Luke and I made a humble feast for two in our city apartment.

I intended to call my grandparents that day, but as the day wore on, time slipped through my fingers like quicksand. I assured myself I would call them in a few days; it didn't seem like a big deal.

However, fate dealt a crushing blow. My grandpa, who had recently received a clean bill of health, suffered a heart attack in his sleep. He was rushed to the hospital and hooked up to a ventilator. Only immediate family members were granted the painful privilege of visiting him, a grim reminder of the pandemic still lurking outside our doors.

I clung desperately to the hope that this was all a dream and that my grandpa would suddenly wake up and everything would return to normal. Yet, I knew in my heart that the reality was far graver.

Throughout the day, my parents relayed updates; each call was like a rollercoaster of hope and despair. In the confines of my apartment, I found myself whispering desperate prayers into the void, "Wake up, Grandpa." I wasn't ready to face a world without him, especially without a proper goodbye.

Then, like a thunderclap on a clear day, my phone rang. An unexpected shiver of apprehension rippled through my body. My mom's voice, usually so full of life, was thick with unshed tears.

"Amber," she choked out, "Grandpa is gone."

The world tilted on its axis.

Sitting hundreds of miles away, I ping-ponged through a whirlwind of emotions - shock, grief, denial. I crumbled to the floor, burning tears streaming down my face. The regret of not making that Thanksgiving call hit me with a renewed force, a bitter reminder of the fleeting nature of time.

"Mom," I whispered into the phone, "It can't be true."

Sadly, it was true.

The man with a zest for life and laughter, who never met a stranger, passed away on November 29, 2020, at Akron General Cleveland Clinic. He was 86. He was a beacon of joy and light in our lives. His infectious laughter could fill a room. He embraced life with open arms, leaving his mark wherever he traveled. He left a legacy of love, laughter, and unforgettable memories.

Note to Self:
Life, like time,
is so very
precious.

Prior to the pandemic, I would have been on the first flight home to attend the funeral. But the health guidelines were clear: non-essential travel was discouraged, and attending a gathering, even one as significant as a funeral, was considered risky.

I was caught in a dilemma. I grappled with choosing between the profound need to say goodbye to my grandfather and the responsibility to protect my family from COVID-19. Every possible scenario played out in my mind.

What if I contracted the virus during travel and unknowingly spread it to my family or others? What if I brought the virus back to New York, further contributing to the city's crisis? What if one day I regretted staying home and not going to the funeral? Each choice seemed to hold its unique heartbreak, and the mental tug-of-war was excruciating.

Finally, after much contemplation, I made the difficult decision to remain in New York and not attend my grandpa's funeral. There was an undeniable sense of guilt and regret coupled with my decision. While not everyone was happy with my decision, I know I made the best decision based on the information I had at the time. In moments of doubt, I took comfort in the certainty that my grandpa, a man of wisdom and understanding, would have respected my decision, even when others questioned it.

I also rationalized that it was better to remember him in the fullness of his life rather than his stillness in death. My grandpa was young at heart and always on the move. His social schedule often seemed busier than mine as he traveled the world, attended car shows, and kept up with his beloved New York Yankees. I strived to be just as active as him in my later years.

* * *

Despite my deep sorrow, I chose not to take bereavement leave from work. I convinced myself that I didn't deserve the time off because I wasn't physically traveling back home. The company had a compassionate bereavement policy in place, acknowledging employees need to tend to their emotional well-being during such difficult times.

When my understanding boss kindly suggested that I take as much time as I needed to mourn and heal, I couldn't accept it. I stubbornly refused to give myself the space away from work to grieve. It was as if I believed that by shouldering everything on my own, I could prove my strength and capability to handle it all. I threw myself into my work, burying my grief beneath a mountain of tasks and deadlines. I neglected my own needs, dismissing the importance of self-care.

Note to Self:
Grief is the
price you pay
for love.

In the weeks following his funeral, I tumbled into a deep depression. I slept a lot and barely had the strength to get out of bed some days. I couldn't fake it anymore—my bubbly, vibrant light had gone out.

I grappled with the realization that funerals are a ceremony for the living - a space to collectively mourn, share memories, and find some semblance of closure. Deprived of this communal grieving process, I felt even more isolated.

When I confided in Luke about my grandpa's death, he suggested I find a therapist. He believed professional guidance could give me the support I needed during this difficult time. I had reservations about therapy due to past experiences that left me feeling more invisible than before. None of these trained experts seemed to resonate with me beyond a few sessions. Thankfully, I was willing to give it one more try.

When I started working with my new therapist Kelly, there was an immediate sense of comfort and trust between us. Her warm and empathetic demeanor created a safe space for me to open up and share my deepest thoughts and emotions. She let me cry, laugh, and let me... be me. Under her compassionate guidance, I embarked on a journey of self-discovery and introspection.

During one of our first sessions, Kelly suggested that I write a letter to my late grandfather to process my grief.

"I know it might seem strange or uncomfortable, but writing a letter can be a powerful way to connect with your emotions and find closure," Kelly said.

I took a moment, like I often did, to pause and let her words sink in.

"I suppose it's worth a try," I said, realizing I had nothing to lose by writing the letter.

"Take your time. There's no rush," she said.

Later that evening, as I procrastinated writing the letter, my pen rolled off my nightstand and onto the floor.

Grandpa, is that you?

As I picked up the pen, I knew what I had to do. I started pouring my thoughts, memories, and unspoken sentiments on paper. It was cathartic like I was having a conversation with him right in my bedroom that night.

Grandpa,

I wish I could tell you in person how much I love you. I miss you so much and would do anything for one of your bear hugs right now. Even though you're gone, I am incredibly grateful we spent as much time together as we did. Thank you for all the love and laughs and for visiting me in NYC.

I am grateful for our hilarious memories together, from you getting "lost" on the way to Tiffany & Co. to you yelling, "Nice boots!" to a young woman walking down the street in Midtown who thought you said something else. (The letters "b" and "t" really do sound very familiar. Ha!)

Grandpa, your voyage may have been cut short, but your legacy sails on in each of us you've loved. Please watch over me. I love you!

– Amber

CHAPTER THREE

The Love Bomb

"Amber, you're a shell of yourself!" Luke's bluntness cut deep. In the weeks following my grandfather's death, I was engulfed by grief. My grandpa was my hero, and his loss left a void no one could fill. Yet Luke's method of addressing my struggle lacked any semblance of softness or empathy. I couldn't help but wonder, did Luke understand the gravity of his words? I ached for understanding and compassion, but Luke seemed unable to fully grasp my sadness.

Luke lost his grandpa around the same time, but he seemed to navigate his sorrow differently. His grief was born from a decades-long journey of watching his grandfather's slow decline. Beneath a "tough guy" façade, Luke, I sensed, wore a mask of stoicism, concealing his emotions. He seemed to mourn quietly. But I couldn't help but wonder why he was so angry with how I dealt with loss. Although his remarks initially made me question whether I should rein in my sadness, I knew my grief was valid, and it was necessary to honor it.

Note to Self:
Healing takes time,
but you will get
through this.

"Can you offer me a little compassion?" I asked.

"Well, you haven't worked out in weeks, and all you want to do is sleep. You aren't yourself," he countered.

While his words were true, I felt so alone. It was as if he was telling me that I didn't know how to grieve correctly. I grew silent. I didn't know what to say, honestly.

Luke gave me a half-apology, saying I took his sentiment the wrong way. But the echo, *You're a shell of yourself*, played like a broken record in my head. I couldn't let it go. My intuition nagged at me, whispering that something was fundamentally wrong.

This was not the first (or last) time Luke said cruel things to me under the guise of being protective and caring. His comments, seemingly harmless on the surface, cut through me. Navigating my relationship became increasingly difficult. He was meant to be my rock during these testing times, but his actions painted a different picture. Instead of offering comfort, he often gave me the impression that my emotions were excessive and my deep sorrow was merely an annoyance to him. Were all relationships a relentless cycle of joy and despair? Was I to blame for our rollercoaster of love?

I tried to excuse his behavior, thinking it was a byproduct of his high-pressure job. As a federal prosecutor, he had the weight of the world on his shoulders with an active role in criminal proceedings. Luke was a real-life superhero putting the "bad guys" away. I admired how he fearlessly tackled some of the city's toughest cases and scariest villains.

Day after day, my boyfriend confronted the darkest corners of humanity; the gravity of his responsibility was beyond my comprehension. This understanding made me more sympathetic, even when his words stung. I recognized he was grappling with his own demons.

I understood that loving someone meant being there through thick and thin, weathering storms together, and emerging stronger on the other side. But lately, I felt like I was running into a fire that Luke started and somehow blaming myself for everything.

Was this a love worth fighting for?

I hesitated to let go. As a woman in my 30s, who had never been married, I questioned whether I had the capacity to love and be loved. Maybe I was expecting too much from the men in my life. But more than anything else, I feared confronting my sense of inadequacy. The questions haunted me. Was I not enough? Was I too much? Was I incapable of being loved?

The love I had for Luke, the shared history, the moments of joy and shared laughter, and the dreams we had woven together all weighed heavily in favor of salvaging what was left. Desperate to make our relationship work, I reminded myself of the joyous moments we shared that had once seemed so abundant. I clung to the hope that these happy times were not mere illusions but the foundation upon which we could rebuild our bond. I just needed to try a little harder.

* * *

From Luke and I's first meeting, his passionate declarations had a hypnotic effect on me.

"You're my soulmate. I've never met anyone like you," Luke said, staring into my eyes.

I fell hard and fast, captivated by the prospect of such profound love, especially when I felt very alone and unwanted.

Two weeks earlier, in the spring of 2018, the media startup I had poured my heart and soul into suddenly went bankrupt. After a full day of work, the CEO casually dropped an email into our inboxes at 5 p.m. It was a cold, impersonal farewell that the company was shutting down, and we needed to empty our desks - effective immediately. Was this even legal? The company, once bustling with energy and potential, seemed to vanish as if it had never existed.

In the following days and weeks, I searched job boards, polished my resume, wrote cover letters, and networked. I remained hopeful that another opportunity would materialize soon. But without a steady income, I had to file for unemployment, which was a humbling experience. Standing in long queues, filling out endless forms, and facing the cold, impersonal bureaucracy reinforced my belief that I was meant for a creative and dynamic career. Yet, it was a crucial lifeline that allowed me to keep my head above water with the city's soaring rent prices.

Although I navigated my days with job hunting, hours-long walks in Central Park, and cheap happy-hour cocktails, I still craved for more genuine connections and companionship. I missed the simple social aspect of having a job, sharing a joke with a colleague, discussing the latest TV show during lunch breaks, or even venting about the quirks of office life. Left in the solitary quiet of my studio apartment, I did what any self-respecting woman in New York would do; I started swiping through my dating apps.

Hey, even if I couldn't find love, I would at least have a free meal, drinks, and a great story to tell my friends. So, precisely sixteen days after losing my job, I met Luke.

Our first date lasted three days, and the intensity of our connection was intoxicating. Quickly, our lives together were a montage of shared adventures and experiences. We explored the world, hiked to majestic waterfalls, and indulged in the best culinary and cultural delights New York City had to offer. We were a couple that embodied spontaneity and zest.

During the whirlwind romance, Luke possessed a remarkable talent for making me feel like the most wonderful woman he'd ever been with. Luke subtly painted his exes as crazy while adding that I was the woman he'd been looking for his whole life. Initially, I saw his openness about past relationships as a symbol of his honesty. I convinced myself that he was naturally charismatic, well-liked, and cherished by everyone. His charisma was one of the many reasons I was drawn to him. He instilled in me the belief that, although he was universally adored, he had singled me out as special, choosing me above all others. I was desperate to feel cherished, to be seen, to be loved.

Two months into dating, Luke asked me to move in with him. I was still jobless, living off unemployment benefits, so the prospect of moving in with Luke presented a silver lining. I could save on rent and be closer to the guy I'd fallen head over heels for.

I packed up my studio in Hell's Kitchen and moved into Luke's condo. Even though alarm bells rang in the recesses of my mind, I chose to ignore them. Moving in together seemed like the fiscally responsible (and incredibly adult) thing to do in NYC.

"High risk. High reward," Luke said.

This phrase quickly became our mantra for all of our big life decisions, especially those others found questionable. We disregarded the cautionary advice, convinced no one else grasped the depth and intensity of our love.

"High risk. High reward," I echoed the day I moved in, convincing myself that the risk was worth the potential happiness ahead. It was only much later that I realized how much of a gamble I was really taking.

The euphoria that came with the early stages of dating slowly waned after I moved in. As we adjusted to sharing our lives under the same roof, the euphoria that came with the early stages of dating waned. Luke's behavior shifted from the overly-attentive boyfriend who made home-cooked meals to a connoisseur of critique. He commented on how I folded the laundry, how I loaded the dishwasher, and even the 'wrong' way I squeezed toothpaste from its tube. It was as if every mundane task I performed was under a microscope. Was this just part of the growing pains of cohabitation?

I didn't want to start a fight, so I simply pushed my feelings down. I loved painting red flags white because I wanted to be the "cool" girl, molding myself into the woman I thought he wanted. My inner people-pleaser went all Elsa from *Frozen* telling me to let it go. So, I did.

Then, one evening, Luke and I went to his best friend Tim's birthday bash. The room was filled with laughter, clinking glasses, and festive chatter. Luke, always the life of the party, mingled and sipped on whiskey. His friends adored him, and honestly, how could they not? He was hilarious, witty, and unabashedly himself. His energetic presence drew everyone in like a magnet, so I was sidelined at the bar, sipping hard cider alone.

Even as the party guests continued to mingle, Luke kept talking and laughing with his long-time friend, Bethenny. Their conversations were filled with inside jokes and shared memories. On any other night, I would have enjoyed their banter, but tonight I felt like a spectator in my own relationship. Knowing I'd just moved in with him, I expected he'd be parading me around. Instead, he wasn't even paying attention to me.

I watched as Luke regaled Bethenny with another one of his stories. Each moment and each laugh that I wasn't a part of stung. When I tried to squeeze my way into their animated conversation, I felt subtly pushed out, like a third wheel. Did they even realize what was happening? Or was I overthinking and turning innocent banter into an insidious plot in my mind?

I wanted to confront him, express my feelings immediately, and demand the attention I deserved. But my good girl persona whispered, "Don't make a scene. You're overreacting."

I smiled and played the part of the perfect girlfriend the rest of the evening, even though, deep down, I was drowning under the weight of my insecurities and doubts about Luke.

Note to Self:
Trust your
intuition.

Thankfully, in the following weeks, I secured a new job and hoped it would help me get out of my funk and focus on something other than Luke's behavior.

"I've got news, Luke. I landed a job," I shared, my voice brimming with excitement and relief.

"Oh," he said.

"Don't act so excited," I joked.

"Well, just be careful, okay? You don't know this company yet," he cautioned. "Did you already take the offer?"

"Yes," I replied, wondering what his hesitation meant.

"I've heard things," he said. "Be careful. You can always back out, you know? You really don't need to work. I can take care of you."

His words hung in the air between us, creating an unsettling tension. Why would he say something like that? Was he implying I had made a poor decision? His lack of enthusiasm left me questioning myself once again.

Soon after starting my new job, Luke was back to monitoring everything I did at home. And it seemed like nothing I did was right, unless I did it his way. He had an opinion on every aspect of my life and wasn't holding back. He didn't like the way I cooked or measured out my ingredients. Then, every morning he commented on the form of my push-ups at the gym - not letting me move forward with a workout until I got it right. He even bought a small kitchen scale to meticulously monitor the calories we consumed.

Note to Self:
Don't change yourself, so other people will like you.

I rationalized that his excessive attention was his way of expressing his care and affection. I truly believed he wanted me to be the best possible version of myself. Also, didn't every relationship require effort and compromise?

Even on the days when I wanted to run away, I found myself reminiscing about those first two magical months we spent together when he adored and validated me. It was challenging to let go of the idea of what our relationship could be. Plus, the thought of leaving was often trumped by a more realistic concern: the daunting financial implications.

NYC is an expensive place to call home. To lease an apartment, most management companies require the first and last month's rent, a security deposit, paperwork verifying employment and current salary (which must be 40x the monthly rent), bank statements, references, and ... well, pretty much everything but your firstborn child.

I did the math, and moving out of Luke's apartment and into a new place would easily set me back at a minimum of $7,500. That kind of financial commitment kept me firmly tethered to his place. I regretted surrendering my studio apartment. But I had moved in with Luke and wanted to prove I could make this relationship work.

In order to do that, I spent more time outside the apartment. Luckily for me, the Pittsburgh Steelers home opener came in the knick of time. The city's Steelers bar was a sight to behold, a sea of black and gold jerseys and a little piece of Pittsburgh right in the heart of Manhattan. It was September 2018.

I was ready to let loose and enjoy myself, away from Luke's critical gaze. I was ready to reconnect with friends I'd known years before I started dating Luke. My crew was in high spirits that afternoon, and each touchdown was met with rowdy cheers, the twirling of Terrible Towels, and a round of Jameson shots. As Wiz Khalifa's "Black and Yellow" blared from the speakers, everyone in the bar began to sing. The whirlwind of revelry, camaraderie, and a Steeler's win left me feeling high. I missed this.

After the game day celebrations ended, I weaved my way home. The world spun around me, and my memory became a smudged canvas. The vibrant black and gold hues of the Steelers' victory were replaced with indistinct blurs due to my overindulgence at the bar.

Thankfully, I made it home in one piece.

The following day, I woke up with a pounding headache, a cruel reminder of the previous night's escapades. But my physical discomfort paled in comparison to the storm of disapproval that awaited me.

"Do you want to apologize for last night? You were blackout drunk," Luke reprimanded me.

His tone was akin to a parent chastising a disobedient child. The shame was discernible, and my cheeks burned with embarrassment.

"I'm so sorry," I said sheepishly. "I had one too many shots. But seriously, was my behavior that bad?"

My memory was a dark void that offered no recollection of what transpired after I crossed the threshold of our apartment. The hazy spaces in my memory only amplified my discomfort, leaving me regretful and confused. Luke raged around the bedroom, and I quickly realized I'd fucked up.

"I was so close to kicking you out of the apartment last night and breaking up with you. But I know you don't have anywhere to go," he roared.

I drank more than my fair share of libations in my life, that much I knew, but the total blackout? It was unsettling, terrifying even. Luke's version of events echoed in my mind. Still, with no memory to cross-reference, it was his story against my vacant recollections.

"Predators are preying on vulnerable, young women like yourself. You could have easily become a target," he told me.

His words were meant to be protective but came off as condescending. Confusion brewed within me as I wondered why my friends had never called out my drinking. *Was I always this monstrous when under the influence?* I berated myself. Until this moment, my assumption had been relatively benign – that I'd staggered home, clumsily found my way to bed, and fell asleep. But Luke's words planted seeds of doubt, challenging my perception of reality. I was left grappling with the unnerving possibility that there was more to the story, a darker side I wasn't privy to. Perhaps after too many libations, I turned into my own Mr. Hyde.

I was left in a cycle of repentance, attempting to make amends for my transgressions. I promised Luke I would abstain from alcohol entirely if it would mend our relationship. Luke dismissed my pleas, comparing me with his ex-girlfriend, whom he claimed was a "crazy" drunk. He also doubted that I could quit alcohol cold turkey.

I decided to quit drinking altogether. I managed to stay sober for thirty days and skipped the next several Steelers games to prove a point, but Luke didn't seem to notice or care. Luke and I's relationship left me dizzy and disoriented. The quirks that made me 'me' gradually faded. But how far was I willing to go to prove I could be loved?

Note to Self:
Give yourself the
love you so easily
give to others.

* * *

As December 2020 approached, the pandemic continued its merciless onslaught, and I was still grieving my grandpa's death. Luke and I went to his family home, nestled in snow-capped mountains, to escape the seemingly incessant claustrophobia and the all-encompassing gloom of New York City. It was like another world.

Each afternoon, we embarked on a hike through the snow-laden wilderness, the crisp air nipping at our cheeks while our boots crunched through the snow. It was magical.

On the third day, Luke was unusually quiet and distant, only glancing my way a few times, a faint smile on his face. The hint of a secret danced in his eyes though. Suddenly, he halted, prompting me to do the same. His gloved hand reached for mine. Before I could question the sudden stop, he dropped to one knee. My heart jolted.

Luke was proposing.

"What are you doing?!" I sputtered, my eyes wide with disbelief.

He had always been a staunch critic of marriage, considering it an antiquated institution, so his actions left me disoriented.

Luke reached into his pocket and flipped open a small box. A gorgeous, vintage diamond ring sparkled in the pale winter sunlight. His eyes locked onto mine.

"I want to spend the rest of my life with you," he confessed, his words echoing in the silent wilderness. "Will you marry me?"

Time stood still as I grappled with the reality unfolding before me. The echo of my heartbeat seemed deafening in the tranquil, snowy wilderness. I stood there, frozen not by the chill in the air but by the sheer magnitude of the moment that was unfolding. I loved this man, and here he was, offering me his heart, life, and future. And then, as if touched by a magic spell, all the worries and questions about our relationship evaporated.

I impulsively leaped into the air, my voice ringing out clear and strong against the peaceful winter landscape, "Yes! I will marry you."

Instantly, the tension etched on Luke's face dissolved.

"Oh my gosh. You scared me there for a minute," he said.

We sealed our newfound promise with a long kiss under the towering pines and amidst the falling snowflakes.

As we stood there, wrapped in each other's arms, a tiny beacon of optimism flickered in my heart, knowing we could find our way. He'd chosen me, and everything felt right in the world.

"Is it okay if I call my parents?" I asked.

Luke nodded, and I reached for my phone, eager to share the news.

I dialed my mom's cell phone, holding my breath as the phone rang, only to be greeted by her voicemail. Frowning, I hung up and tried again, but to no avail. My heart sank a little. Then, a text appeared on the screen: "At Giant Eagle, will call you later."

I blinked at the message. My initial disappointment gave way to an amused chuckle. I was freshly engaged in the middle of a winter wonderland, and my parents were grocery shopping. They must not have known Luke was planning to propose. Was it old-fashioned to wish for the traditional route, where the proposer asks for the parents' blessing beforehand? Did it even matter in this day and age?

There I go overthinking again.

I slipped the phone back into my pocket and turned to Luke. The news could wait. For now, it was just the two of us.

"I can't wait to spend the rest of my life with you," I said.

His eyes lit up as he pulled me closer. His lips met mine again in a sweet, lingering kiss that held the promise of our shared future.

Pulling back, he held my gaze.

"I love you, Amber James," he said.

We spent the rest of the hike, basking in that new engagement glow.

* * *

I finally got in touch with my parents later that day. As the video chat connected, I held my hand up, the diamond ring sparkling under the soft light.

"We're engaged!" I said, beaming.

They congratulated me, but their happiness seemed restrained. I couldn't blame them; I'd been engaged before, but it hadn't worked out. My heart twinged at the thought, but I brushed it off. This time, it would be different.

Next, I called my grandma. As soon as our FaceTime call connected, her eyes lit up, and she immediately spotted the ring adorning my finger.

"What a beautiful ring!" she exclaimed.

Her excitement was contagious, and I couldn't help but smile from ear to ear. I shared the story of Luke's proposal and how he had surprised me during our hike.

My grandmother listened intently, her eyes filled with joy and love.

"You deserve every bit of happiness," she said, her voice filled with warmth. While left unsaid, our engagement served as a ray of sunshine piercing through the clouds that had loomed over us following my grandfather's passing.

When we finally announced our engagement on Facebook, the response was overwhelming. The heartfelt comments poured in, turning the post into one of the most 'liked' photos I'd ever shared; it came in second to me meeting my teenage crush Joshua Jackson, who played the hilariously sarcastic rebel Pacey Witter on *Dawson's Creek*. (Team Pacey forever!)

The intoxicating high we were riding on gently receded. Gradually, we found ourselves returning to the sobering rhythms of our everyday life, revealing the path of shared responsibilities and lifelong commitment that lay ahead. The joy was still present, but with it came a profound understanding of what our 'Yes' truly meant. The weight of expectations and societal pressures began to encroach upon our relationship. I felt the need to meet specific standards to please Luke and paint our relationship as perfect to all our family and friends. Driven to be the "perfect" wife-to-be,

I put immense pressure on myself, striving to meet every demand and surpass every standard.

Despite the commitment symbolized by our engagement, I couldn't shake off the unsettling feeling that I was still contending for his love. There was this lurking fear that a single slip-up, a single moment of not meeting his expectations, could result in him walking away, leaving behind our promises to each other. So, I decided to bring up my internal struggles with my therapist.

"My brain is going a hundred miles per hour," I admitted, rolling through the list of questionable interactions I had with Luke. "Am I to blame for this?"

"Well, how does it feel when your fiancé says you're a shell of yourself?" my therapist Kelly asked me. (*See, I told you I couldn't let it go!*)

"Hurt and broken, as if I'll never make him happy. No matter how hard I try. I am beginning to question everything like, am even worthy of love?" I sighed.

It was liberating and eye-opening to vocalize the confusion that had been simmering within me for far too long. Opening up to Kelly provided a safe space to express my deepest fears, doubts, and uncertainties and let out a good ugly cry.

"Amber, I want you to know that you are worthy of love - as you are right now," she said. "Someone else's validation or approval does not determine your worthiness." Her words struck a chord within me, shifting the focus from

Luke and spotlighting the journey of healing I needed to embark on. It forced me to question why I could not extend the same level of love and compassion to myself that I so freely offered to others. I had become my adversary, trapped in the relentless pursuit of pleasing others and seeking validation from the outside world to feel valued.

"The world is undoubtedly brighter with you in it. You have a big heart, and I am so honored to be able to come into this space and work with you every week," Kelly said as I continued to take in all the information.

"I needed to hear that," I confessed. "I can be incredibly hard on myself. I need to be kinder and more compassionate."

Though it was easier said than done, I was committed to creating a loving relationship with my beautifully imperfect self.

CHAPTER FOUR

A Race Against Time

Doubled over the porcelain toilet, I expelled the remnants of everything I had ingested that day. As the unpleasant ordeal continued, I wondered if I had food poisoning. I mentally listed all the food I'd consumed that day: an oat milk latte, a toasted English muffin, and scrambled eggs. I wandered into the kitchen to scrutinize the expiration dates on the food items. All seemed in order, so what was wrong with me?

Despite my best efforts to sleep off the excruciating discomfort and rest, the pain was intensifying. I put off going to the emergency room, fearing the doctors would dismiss my symptoms as psychosomatic and all "in my head." You see, for over ten years, I'd been grappling with persistent digestive issues. Many doctors had brushed off my bloating, indigestion, and weight gain as mere side effects of growing older and being a woman. The parade of doctors I visited had a host of theories for my symptoms, prescribing treatments, medications, and lifestyle changes that only offered fleeting relief, if any. One practitioner even prescribed yoga and an enema. These experiences left me questioning my own judgment and pain tolerance.

But at around 5 p.m. that evening, a sudden surge of pain in my lower abdomen brought me to my knees. It was an agony impossible to ignore. I had to go to the emergency room, even during a pandemic.

Note to Self:
Listen to
your body.

Luke had recently resumed his in-office working routine, so I texted him about my situation and my imminent trip to the ER. I reassured him that I would keep him updated as the situation unfolded.

His reply was instant, a clear demonstration of his concern. He urged me to stay safe and promised to keep his phone nearby. All the hospitals in NYC were restricting visitors to help reduce exposure to COVID-19, so I told him not to rush home. I had to go through this one alone.

I hastily gathered the essential items -my phone, purse, health insurance card, mask, ID, and house keys -and walked out the door. Each step made me wince in pain, so I opened my Uber app. The estimated wait time exceeded twenty minutes - a virtual lifetime in my current state. *Was the car in another time zone?!*

Full of adrenaline and pure frustration, I started walking to the emergency room on foot. (It was less than a mile away. I could do it.) I began establishing minor targets to distract myself from the piercing pain. First, I aimed to reach the blue Mini Cooper parked just ahead. Then, I set my sights on the brick townhouse a little further down the street.

Next, it was the stop sign that loomed in the distance. This pattern of goal-setting continued throughout the mile-long trek. But with each step, the pain in my side intensified, making it clear I had underestimated the toll this journey would take on me. I hadn't accounted for the frequent pauses to regain my breath or the slowed pace due to the crippling pain.

Eventually, after what felt like an eternity (but was likely only fifteen minutes), I stumbled through the sliding doors of the hospital's emergency room. I conveyed to the intake nurse through gritted teeth that I was experiencing severe pain in my lower right abdomen. Another nurse, previously engrossed at his computer, shot up from his seat and zipped over to me. You could see the worry in his eyes as he started grilling me about my symptoms.

"Sounds like appendicitis," he said with urgency. "She needs to get a CT scan."

Despite the waiting area being inundated with patients, I was promptly escorted into the emergency room bay. It was 6:13 p.m.

Oh, shit. This is serious.

After changing into a gown and getting my paperwork in order, I was rolled onto another floor for my CT scan, which would confirm if I had appendicitis.

I knew we were in a race against time, but minutes turned to hours as I waited for the results. The wait likely had to do with all the drama unfolding in the emergency room; it held my undivided attention like a TV show. I caught glimpses of various characters through a narrow gap in the curtains. A paramedic spoke to a 40-something man who allegedly cheated death after overdosing. He claimed that he only indulged on his birthday. Far from being amused, the paramedic retorted, "That's what you told us last week."

Close by, a female patient was causing a ruckus, hurling expletives at the hospital staff. Her agitation was intense. She banged her fists against the metal bed frame, adding an unsettling soundtrack to an already tense environment.

My gaze then shifted toward a scene that could easily have been lifted straight out of a movie. A man in his thirties donned a white shirt covered in blood. He was being diligently attended to by a team of medical professionals. The scene was oddly cinematic. And yet, this was no film – this was a real person, in real pain, experiencing the very real consequences of violence.

These snippets of lives in crisis captivated me for hours until a doctor's voice broke through.

"Confirmed! She has acute appendicitis. Administer morphine and antibiotics," he ordered.

By now, it was nearly 9 p.m., so I called Luke, updating him on my situation. When I delivered the news that I'd be undergoing surgery in a few hours, Luke replied, "I wish I could be there with you."

"I wish you could be here, too," I said.

Given the hospital's restrictions, he was not allowed to visit until the following day.

Luke sighed.

"When, you're out of surgery, call me, okay? Even if it's the middle of the night. I'll be waiting," he said.

"I will, Luke," I promised. "I love you."

"I love you, too, Amber," he said.

Waves of sharp, stabbing sensations relentlessly pierced my abdomen, which according to one nurse, was a "good sign," indicating my appendix had not yet burst.

The next few hours were a blur, with pain medication administered via an IV and a barrage of questions thrown my way. It felt as if I was under interrogation.

"Do you have a living will?" a medical assistant casually inquired. I responded with a nervous laugh; this was my typical reaction when stressed.

"No," I answered. "Should I have one? Is it too late?"

The assistant smiled, instructing me to mark 'No' on the pin pad. Amidst this flurry, I provided a copayment and credit card information while clad in only a hospital gown.

Around midnight, nearly six hours after arriving at the hospital, I was moved into a pre-surgery area, where I met my surgeon, Dr. Savage. He applied pressure to a spot above my appendix as he inquired about my pain. An intense surge of agony jolted through my body, causing me to involuntary jump. Curse words burst from my lips.

"F**k!" I yelped.

"I'm so sorry. We will take care good care of you. Trust me, you're in good hands with this team," Dr. Savage reassured me.

The nurse Sarah was a beacon of light in this chaotic ordeal. She equipped me with a "party hat" (disposable hair cap) and "go-go boots" (compression stockings), while another nurse presented a pre-surgery "cocktail" (a potent mix of medication). For the first time that day, I breathed a sigh of relief. I was transported into the operating room and succumbed to an anesthesia-induced oblivion.

When I woke in recovery around 2:30 a.m., the nurse told me it was a good thing I didn't wait a second longer to come to the emergency room.

Gangrene had already set in - meaning my appendix was close to rupturing. They removed my organ in the nick of time, avoiding widespread infection, abscess, sepsis, and even death.

Note to Self:
Advocate for yourself. It may save your life.

"Can you call my fiancé and tell him I'm okay?" I asked the attending nurse.

She picked up the nearby phone and called Luke. I heard her tell him the details and that I was in recovery.

"He says he loves you," she relayed to me.

"I love him, too," I said.

As I lay in my hospital bed, tethered to an array of IVs, I realized that suffering in silence could have had fatal consequences. This chilling revelation served as a sobering wake-up call about the fragility of life. I pledged then and there to embrace each moment, express my feelings more openly, and ask for help when needed.

With a renewed perspective, I was ready to embrace life in all its messy, beautiful complexity. I was determined to seek experiences that challenged and fueled my growth. I would savor each moment, the good and the bad. I promised myself to take risks and step out of my comfort zone, even if they frightened me. I would not merely exist but live fully, deeply, and consciously. After all, we get one shot at this life, and I was determined to make it count.

CHAPTER FIVE

The Scars You Can't See

Those first few weeks after surgery were challenging. I spent most of my time sleeping, trying to regain my strength. Luke took it upon himself to be my caretaker. At first, I appreciated his willingness to support me and thought it would bring us closer together. However, as the days turned into weeks, I couldn't help but sense Luke's growing resentment of my dependency on him. Although we were heading toward a commitment to love each other "in sickness and in health," Luke seemed to be withdrawing from me.

In response, I pushed myself to do household tasks like laundry, cleaning, and cooking, even though I had little energy. I desperately wanted to prove I could do things on my own and didn't need a caretaker.

"I can handle this, you know," I remember telling him one morning, even as I struggled to carry the laundry basket.

So he pulled back just like I'd asked him.

Now, instead of being present at home, Luke spent more time at the office, leaving me feeling utterly alone in the relationship, literally and physically.

Even though I was working from home, the days of solitude in the apartment gave way to so much overthinking. I began overanalyzing the savage, purple scars crisscrossing my swollen abdomen - souvenirs from the laparoscopic appendectomy. These were harsh reminders etched into my skin of the ordeal my body had endured.

I traced the jagged lines with my fingers, each one a stark contrast against my bloated belly.

Note to Self:
You're perfect
just the way
you are.

These physical scars greatly affected my self-esteem, causing me to grapple with a distorted image of my body. Questions and doubts crept in, festering in my mind, making me wonder if I could ever measure up to the woman I was before the surgery. These were the hidden wounds and unspoken fears that gnawed at me, adding another dimension of pain harder to heal than any physical scar.

While I hated being alone, my inadequacy grew deeper when Luke and I were together. Suddenly, all his conversations were about his work and his new co-worker, Crystal. His infatuation with her was obvious, and it crushed me. I didn't want to be the jealous girlfriend, but he talked about her daily.

I thought I was going crazy, so I tracked every time he mentioned her. To my dismay, the count reached ten times within a twenty-four-hour period. Gross. If my scars were not enough to break my self-confidence, the way Luke spoke about Crystal did.

"Luke, you mention her quite often," I blurted out.

"Really?" He looked genuinely surprised. "Do I bring her up too much?"

"More than you realize. And it hurts me," I confessed, a lump forming in my throat.

"Oh, come on, Amber. Don't be so jealous," he retorted dismissively.

The label "jealous" struck a nerve. It hurt. But before I could respond, Luke was off on another tangent.

"Look, I know you told me not to talk about her, but you've got to hear this story," he continued, disregarding my discomfort.

Overwhelmed with frustration and anger, I felt at a loss for how to articulate my feelings any clearer. It seemed as though my heartfelt confessions were falling on deaf ears. As I wrestled with my simmering jealousy, I consciously directed my attention toward a new beacon of hope: the COVID-19 vaccine was finally available for U.S. citizens in my age bracket.

Finding an appointment, though, became a quest of its own, a maddening maze of online portals and endless refreshes. I scoured multiple websites day and night until I finally discovered an elusive opening. I seized it, filling in the necessary information and securing my spot. With bated breath, I clicked the final button to confirm my appointment, praying and waiting for the confirmation screen to appear. Relief washed over me as the confirmation email landed in my inbox.

On the day of the appointment, I stood outside a towering renowned hospital in Lower Manhattan. The line snaked along the busy sidewalk filled with fellow New Yorkers eager for their shot of protection. Anxiety and anticipation filled the air; we all understood the significance of this moment. My heart and mind raced with excitement and questions. Would the vaccine live up to its promises? Would this be the key to reclaiming some semblance of normalcy for us? Although the vaccine's long-term effects were unknown, I was willing to take that risk to safeguard myself and others from the virus.

As my turn arrived, a sense of relief washed over me. I watched the syringe empty, knowing this simple act was a crucial step in the fight against the pandemic.

I had renewed sense of gratitude for the scientists, healthcare professionals, and countless unsung heroes who had worked tirelessly to develop, distribute, and administer the vaccine.

I could finally breathe a little easier for the first time in over a year.

Following the vaccination, I received my vaccination card, which served as a tangible verification of this pivotal moment. It bore the date of my first shot and clear instructions that I needed to return for the second dose. It was a commitment I embraced, knowing that the vaccine's full benefits would be realized with the completion of the two-shot regimen.

Over the next 24 hours, a mild fever crept in, accompanied by a general feeling of fatigue. It was a small price to pay for the protection the vaccine offered. I took it as a sign that my body was mounting a defense against the virus and building immunity that would safeguard me.

When I finally received my second shot, I was empowered to navigate the world without fear and felt secure enough to board an airplane. I was ready to see my family. So when I got home, I logged online to book a flight. I asked Luke if he wanted to join me, but he claimed he couldn't take time off because he and Crystal were working on a major case. His response pierced through my heart like a dagger. I understood the demands of his job, but I wanted him with me. Was it a bad sign that he couldn't take time off to accompany me? Or was it just a coincidence that he had a lot of work to do? I pushed those thoughts aside, hoping our time apart could give us some breathing room to get our relationship back on track.

Absence makes the heart grow stronger... right?

* * *

As I walked through the airport, the air buzzed with excitement and anticipation. Every step carried me closer to the long-awaited reunion with my family. I could hardly contain the joy bubbling within me.

When I spotted my parents, I rushed to them. As we embraced, I could feel their warmth and love envelop me. We stood there momentarily, relishing the joy of being together again. How had we managed to go a year without hugging one another? I didn't want to let go.

The 45-minute drive home flew by as if time couldn't wait for us to be home. When we pulled into the driveway, the familiar sight of our house filled me with comfort and belonging. It felt so damn good to be back.

There would be so many emotions in the coming days, primarily good ones, but I also knew my homecoming had a bittersweet undertone. I would finally face the reality of my grandpa's death.

* * *

I hugged myself tightly, trying to ward off the bone-chilling cold while looking at the headstone before me. It all felt dreamlike. Here I was, standing at my grandpa's grave.

His final resting place faced the nearby Harry Clever Field Airport runway, a deliberate decision he made. The thought of him watching the planes taking off and landing, even in the realm beyond, brought a bittersweet smile to my face. It was a testament to his free spirit and endearing love for aircraft.

I was quiet on the outside, but inside, I was having a full-blown conversation with my grandpa. I told him everything — how much I missed him and how I wanted to make him proud. It was a one-way chat, but it made me feel like maybe he could hear me. Like he was still there, looking out for me.

I wished Luke could've been there at that moment to hold me. But then, I realized I had an even better source of support - my dad, always steady and understanding, ready to lend a shoulder when I needed it the most.

"I miss him," I confessed.

My dad's reply mirrored my sentiments, "Me too."

After soaking in a few more moments of quiet remembrance, I suggested a change of scenery.

"Can we visit grandma? I'd like to stop by her house," I proposed.

And so, we did just that.

When we arrived, my grandpa's absence struck me even harder. My eyes kept darting around the familiar space, half-expecting him to saunter around the corner at any moment, his face lighting up as he'd say, "There's our New York City girl."

The house felt hollow without him. The longer I sat there, the more the bitter reality of his death hit me. I would never again see his warm smile, hear his hearty laughter, or feel his comforting bear hugs.

I tried to put on a brave face in front of my grandma, but the pent-up emotions inside me were too strong. The tears I had been holding back for months finally cascaded down my cheeks. It was a much-needed release and perhaps my first real step towards accepting and coping with my grandpa's death.

In that moment of profound sadness, though, I still had my grandma. She was here, and we had a lifetime of new adventures and joyous moments awaiting us. It was time to be fully present for her, to cherish our time together, and ensure that I wouldn't let so much time pass before seeing her again.

After my glorious ugly cry, I resolved to do whatever it took to be closer to my family and bridge the physical distance that had separated us for far too long.

* * *

Later that afternoon, I reached for my phone. My thumb hovered over Luke's name; I was ready to tell him about my emotional day. After all, love wasn't just about sharing joy; it was also about leaning on each other during times of sorrow.

"Hey there! Just wanted to check in and see how your day's been," I greeted him.

"It's been good, busy as usual," Luke replied.

"What are you getting into tonight?" I asked, assuming he'd be playing video games in his pajamas.

"Actually, Crystal's coming over to the apartment. We're going to have a cocktail here and then go to Nino's for some food. We thought it would be a great way to unwind after this crazy week," he said.

"W-Why is she coming over to our apartment?" I stammered. My voice was a mix of confusion and concern.

"We wanted to hang out. It's just a casual thing, nothing to worry about," Luke responded.

I was silent. I honestly didn't know what to say.

"What's wrong?" he asked.

"I think it's weird that she's coming over to our apartment while I'm away," I said. "And... that I've never met her."

"Oh, babe. She's just a friend," he said.

I stayed silent.

"Oh my gosh, don't put your unresolved jealousy from your previous relationship on me. I'm not a cheater like ex-boyfriend Dax," he added.

Where did that come from? What did my ex have to do with Crystal coming to our apartment?

My thoughts were in overdrive. Could it be possible that Luke was leveraging the intimate details I'd shared about my past relationships to his advantage?

"Crystal understands parts of my job that I don't want to bring home to you," he explained. "Trust me, when you get back, you can meet Crystal. I'm sure you'll love her."

His words struck a nerve. *I'll love her?*

"Well, it's weird. I don't get it," I said.

"Amber, don't worry. I love you. You're my person," he said sweetly.

Luke brought up the teachings of Esther Perel, a renowned relationship expert. Perel often speaks about how we now rely on one individual to provide what used to be fulfilled by an entire village. This concept became Luke's rationale for needing Crystal's presence in his life. He claimed that he didn't want to burden me with the responsibility of being his 'entire village.' He wanted to distribute that load, and Crystal was a part of that system. His words held some truth, leading me to question if I was overanalyzing things.

"Well, have fun. Let's chat tomorrow. I love you," I said.

As soon as the call ended, I bolted outside. Tears gushed from my eyes leaving behind streaks of mascara. My chest tightened as if somebody had punched me. I couldn't breathe.

As luck would have it, my brother was pulling up in his car. I hadn't planned on encountering anyone; all I wanted was to retreat into solitude.

My brother walked over to me with an expression of genuine concern etched on his face.

"What happened? Are you okay?" he asked.

I wiped my eyes and tried to steady my voice, "It's Luke. He...he's been spending time with his new female co-worker. And now she's coming to our apartment tonight while I'm here," I explained.

"I should be okay with it, but it also feels like he's relying on this woman more than he should. It just hurts. Am I crazy to be upset about this?" I asked

"First off, you are not crazy. This situation is odd," my brother said, bringing me in for a hug.

He inquired further. "So he's still hanging out with her even after you expressed concern?"

"Yeah," I said weakly.

Over the years, our conversations usually skimmed the surface of everyday life, steering clear of the deeper emotional currents. However, this simple exchange and his validation of my feelings held a significance that far outweighed any previous discussion.

My brother had my back, and I didn't just feel heard; I felt seen.

* * *

When I sent a message to Luke later that evening, he didn't respond. My temper rose to an inferno. He always had his phone on him. Why was he not texting me back?!

I couldn't help but wonder what he and Crystal could be doing that he couldn't spare a moment to respond to me. When Luke and I were together, he seemed to have time to text her or take her calls. I couldn't shake the feelings of betrayal coursing through my veins. I was infuriated as I waited for a response that didn't come.

My eyes remained locked on the screen of my phone, watching the minutes turn into hours. It wasn't until the sun peeked over the horizon, ushering in a new day, that I finally connected with him over the phone.

Fueled by my own pain, I had sought to inflict a similar hurt upon him. So before he could get a word in, I erupted.

"Are you sleeping with Crystal? What's happening between you two?!" My voice was seething with pent-up resentment and anger.

Regret washed over me as I acknowledged the gravity of my accusations, but it was too late to take them back.

"Whoa. Whoa. Nothing is happening, Amber," he replied, "Chill."

I had zero chill.

Luke tried to address my fears, but I barely registered his words. My intuition insisted there was more to this "friendship," but I couldn't prove it. For now, I had to take his word for it.

* * *

When I returned to New York, Luke and I tried to sift through our complicated mess of miscommunication and distrust.

"So, where do we go from here?" he inquired.

"I need to be honest with you, Luke. It has been bothering me how much you talk about Crystal. It makes me uncomfortable, and sometimes it feels like you're infatuated with her," I confessed.

"I'm sorry if it comes across that way, but Crystal and I are just friends," he said.

"It's not just about romantic feelings. I also feel uneasy about having people I've never met in our apartment. I value our privacy. I mean, seriously, would you want me to bring a guy - you'd never met - over here while you were out of town?" I asked.

"Honestly, I wouldn't care," he retorted. "I trust you."

I had naively expected him to grovel at my feet, pleading for forgiveness with his tail between his legs. I hoped my fiancé would apologize and say he'd stop hanging out with her for the sake of our relationship. For the next few hours, our conversation seemed caught in an endless loop, circling around the same points without making any meaningful progress. Then came the bombshell.

"I guess I am trying to figure out my feelings for Crystal," he said.

His sudden confession gave me emotional whiplash.

"What?!" I snapped.

The man, whose affections I thought were exclusively mine, had just tossed a grenade into our fragile relationship. How could Luke even consider having feelings for someone else when we were engaged? All the memories we had built together suddenly felt like they meant nothing to him.

When he noticed the stunned look on my face, he quickly added, "I didn't mean romantically. I love you, and you will always be my number one. You're my soulmate. You know that."

Luke insisted that Crystal posed no threat to our relationship; instead, he saw her presence as a contribution to our lives. He tried to reassure me that there was nothing to be worried about, even proposing the idea of the three of us hanging out together.

Although his words were likely meant to alleviate my lingering doubts, I still felt baffled and hurt.

"I can't keep you from hanging out with her because she is your co-worker, but I'd appreciate it if you cooled down the hanging out without me," I said.

"Oh, so you're trying to say I can't have female friends?" he asked. "You're so jealous and controlling."

I knew I deserved better, but I felt utterly paralyzed. Maybe, I was the problem. My jealousy and lack of trust were on full display; I felt so shameful about it. I secretly wished the emotional pain could become a physical bruise, providing undeniable evidence for why it was necessary to leave.

While I contemplated the uncertain future of our relationship, Luke abruptly changed the subject.

"Do you want to get sushi?" he asked.

His off-topic query about dinner left me dumbfounded as if he were deliberately evading the discussion with a blatant disregard for its importance. Was he genuinely reaching out with an olive branch or merely playing another hand in this emotional game?

"You want to get sushi... right now?" I asked.

"I think we could use a break. Don't you think? I want to spend some time with you," he said.

His sweet tone made my heart melt. Maybe he wasn't trying to hurt me with his female friendships. I needed to stop being so jealous.

I gave in and agreed to the impromptu sushi date. I embraced the possibility that, for a few fleeting hours, the magic of this shared experience could reignite our love. But there was also a quiet desire to prove that I could fulfill Luke's needs and render Crystal irrelevant. And it would start over a fifteen-course sushi omakase dinner.

CHAPTER SIX

Notes To Self

Luke and I were still at an impasse after sushi, unable to find common ground regarding his relationship with Crystal. He was insistent about maintaining that friendship, so I had two choices - I had to end the relationship or let Luke have his way. I hated both options.

Looking for a way to escape my analysis paralysis, I turned to my stack of Post-It notes. At the very least, I could work on boosting my self-esteem and injecting positivity into the apartment, which felt saturated with negativity and tension. I picked up a pen and began to write. On one note, I affirmed, "I am beautiful."

The uplifting messages made me feel better, so I wrote more of them. The vibrant collection of sticky notes - in pink, blue, red, yellow, and purple hues - lifted my spirits while subtly reinforcing my sense of resilience and strength.

I stuck the notes all around - on the refrigerator door, the bathroom mirror, the coffee machine, and even in my sock drawer. I could feel a subtle shift in my mood. These tiny, colorful squares, filled with affirmations, pearls of wisdom, gentle reminders, and comforting messages, were making a positive difference.

Note to Self:
One positive
thought can
change your day.

Then, it occurred to me that if these notes could bring so much light into my life, couldn't they do the same for others? I knew the most effective way to spread these messages was through social media. I opted for Instagram, choosing the handle @NotesToSelfShop.

I had one goal: to bring positivity and hope to anyone struggling and needing a quick boost. Within weeks, the page took off, reaching thousands of people.

Messages poured in from all corners of the world, and each person shared their unique story of how my notes resonated with them. I couldn't believe the affirmations that had started as my personal source of strength now offered comfort and inspiration to others. I had tapped into something meaningful. And this was just the beginning.

CHAPTER SEVEN

Another Organ Bites the Dust

Unbearable pain surged beneath my ribcage as the subway car swayed rhythmically along the tracks. Every rattle seemed to jolt through my body. While it didn't warrant a frantic dash to the ER, I wondered if this pain was linked to my recent surgery.

When the subway grumbled to a stop at my station, I took a deep breath. I disembarked, emerging from the cavernous depths of the subway near Sixth Avenue. My thoughts drowned out the city's bustling noises.

I knew if anyone could help me, it was Dr. Savage. He wasn't just a doctor to me; he was the surgeon who had saved my life, so my trust in him was unwavering.

I ducked into the first bodega I saw, hoping it would offer a break from the noisy city. I dialed Dr. Savage's office, each ring echoing my escalating anxiety. Finally, the receptionist's cheerful voice broke through my contemplation.

"Dr. Savage's office. How can I assist you today?" she said.

I quickly explained my new gnawing symptoms, mentioning my recent appendectomy. I asked if the doctor could fit me into his schedule.

"Someone just canceled. Can you come at 3:45 p.m. today?" she asked.

"I'll be there," I replied, knowing I needed answers.

* * *

After I checked in with the front desk, I was escorted through the sterile halls of the doctor's office and led to a private room. Dr. Savage entered. His white coat billowed as he walked briskly toward me with a smile.

"How are you feeling?" he asked, likely out of habit.

I started explaining my ordeal, attempting to convey the severity of my pain. He seemed genuinely attentive, probing further with questions.

"My gut reaction - without running any tests - is that it might be your gallbladder. Have you ever had it checked to see if it is functioning properly or if you have gallstones?" he inquired.

I shook my head, "Nope."

"Okay, we need to conduct a few tests first," the doctor said. "But we'll get to the bottom of this."

His words, though measured and professional, offered a ray of hope. He explained the tests included an ultrasound and a hepatobiliary iminodiacetic acid (HIDA) scan.

The HIDA scan involved injecting a radioactive tracer into the veins, which makes the gallbladder contract and empty. Meanwhile, a gamma camera is positioned over the abdomen to take pictures of the tracer as it moves through the body.

As he explained the test, I felt like a subject of a transformative experiment, something straight out of an X-Men comic. I couldn't help but play with the idea: would I emerge from this experience as a superhero with extraordinary powers?

"Let's do it," I said.

*   *   *

The ultrasound procedure felt eerily similar to the ones I'd seen on television, where expecting mothers gaze at the screen with wide-eyed wonder, watching the image of their unborn child. Except in my case, the object of interest wasn't a baby but my gallbladder.

The female technician carefully spread the cool, clear gel on my abdomen. Its chill made me wince. As she moved the probe gently across my skin, I watched the grey, fuzzy images on the screen. I tried deciphering the blobs and shadows, but they were an enigma to my untrained eye.

"I'm not finding anything out of the ordinary," she said, her voice calm and even. "Your gallbladder looks normal on the ultrasound."

"Normal" was good but didn't explain my pain. If the ultrasound was clear, then what was causing my discomfort?

Noticing the confusion on my face, she said, "We're not done yet. Given your symptoms, Dr. Savage has also recommended a HIDA scan. It's a more specific test to assess gallbladder function."

With that, I was ushered out of the ultrasound room and onto the next phase of this wild health journey, armed with a referral slip. It was like I was on an endless quest for answers. The pain was real, but the source was elusive. I couldn't help but think, something has got to give!

As I pushed open the door to the Radiology department, I took a deep, steadying breath, readying myself for the next test.

My heart fluttered with anxiety when the attending technician outlined the procedure of the HIDA scan, which would be a two-hour diagnostic marathon requiring me to remain still.

"Don't move, or we'll have to start over," she warned.

Faced with the daunting task of staying motionless, I tried to distract myself, but the walls felt like they were caving in on me. All I wanted to do was move my body.

The nurse gently suggested sleeping through the test, likely sensing my mounting anxiety. However, I worried about accidentally stirring and disrupting the results.

Note to Self:
Breathe.
Everything
will be okay.

Finally, at the ninety-minute mark, with the finish line in sight, I tried to engage the nurse in casual conversation.

"How's it looking?" I asked.

Legally, she was bound to silence, but her facial expression told me everything I needed to know. My gallbladder was coming out.

Days later, Dr. Savage confirmed what I already knew.

"We need to remove your gallbladder as soon as possible," he said.

So less than two months after my appendectomy, I was back in the hospital, facing another surgery and losing another organ.

* * *

"Time to wake up, Amber. Welcome to recovery," a warm voice said, coaxing me from the foggy remnants of anesthesia.

I slowly regained consciousness after my cholecystectomy (gallbladder removal surgery), still disorientated.

"How are you feeling? Can you tell me where you are on the pain scale—like one, meaning no pain, or ten, meaning excruciating pain?" the nurse asked me.

"Ten or eleven," I mumbled, the words coming out slow and slurred. "When... when will I get pain meds?"

The nurse's eyes filled with concern.

"You've already been given pain medication, Amber," she said.

The knowledge only sparked more confusion. Why was my pain so agonizing?

"What did you give me? Tylenol?" I blurt out. (The anesthesia, which was still clouding my judgment, bore the blame for my senseless chatter.)

"We've been giving you Fentanyl," the nurse replied.

I let out an audible gasp as I processed what she said. All I knew about the synthetic opioid was what I heard on the news: Americans were overdosing on drugs laced with Fentanyl. The drug would be much different in a medical setting than in an illicit drug market, but that didn't make it any less scary.

The persistent pain was overwhelming, making every movement a struggle. I felt incredibly fragile. It was a far cry from the reprieve I had hoped the operation would provide.

The nurse returned to my side and injected more medication into my IV.

"Give it a few minutes. It should start working soon," she said.

The painkillers were potent, engineered to numb even the most excruciating of pains, and yet, they seemed to have little effect on me.

I was desperate for any relief, so I closed my eyes and fell asleep. I wondered if it might be easier just to die.

When I woke again, my discomfort had decreased just enough for me to stop voicing complaints. All I wanted was to be at home, resting in my own bed.

"Good news," the nurse said, waving my discharge papers. "You can go home now."

She reviewed the instructions on post-operative care and prescriptions for painkillers. Thankfully, Luke was there to take notes because I wasn't in any state to remember what she said.

"Remember to rest and keep hydrated," she reminded, her voice soft yet firm. "And don't hesitate to call us if the pain persists."

* * *

When we arrived home, Luke returned to his role as the caregiver. He cooked meals, ensured I took my medication, and fluffed my pillows even though I didn't ask him to. From an outsider's perspective, he was the perfect partner, caring for my needs. But with every act of service, I felt like I was accumulating a debt that I'd have to repay later. Luke was physically by my side, providing the practical support I desperately needed, but there was a noticeable distance between us.

In the days and weeks that followed my surgery, Luke's time at work increased, and his presence at home dwindled. Weekends, once our shared refuge, were now spent at the office assisting Crystal with her cases. And when he was home, she was the topic of conversation as he regaled stories about how smart and incredible she was in court. He even casually admitted, as if it were the most normal thing in the world, that he had bought her a massage, handpicked books for her to read, and brought her favorite flavor of ice cream to work.

My self-esteem took a hit, and his growing infatuation with her didn't help. It seemed as if he was moving forward with his life while I was in a purgatory of recovery that was taking way longer than I anticipated. I tried to bottle up my inner turmoil, but I knew these emotions, if not carefully released, were akin to a ticking time bomb. So, one evening while under the influence of my prescribed painkillers, I mustered the courage to talk to Luke.

"Luke, there is something weighing heavily on my mind, or rather, someone," I conveyed.

Before I uttered the next word, a sigh escaped his lips.

"Crystal?" he asked.

Her name hung in the air between us.

"Why are we bringing her up again, Amber?" Luke asked.

"When you spend time with her, bring her up over dinner, or share things with her about our relationship, it stirs up feelings of insecurity within me," I confessed.

I thought I was safe expressing my vulnerability with Luke and trusted that he would receive my fears with understanding and compassion. But I was wrong.

"Amber, I'm not like your past relationships. I'm not being unfaithful," he said with frustration creeping into his voice. "Why are you so jealous?"

"You're sharing more than just work hours with her," I voiced.

"I don't know how many times I have to tell you, but we're just friends. Nothing more," he said.

His words, meant to reassure me, only fed into my growing insecurities. Luke's actions were causing me to question everything - his respect for me, his commitment to our relationship, and his boundaries at work.

I knew I deserved better but didn't yet have the strength to mentally or physically walk away from the toxicity. The thought of navigating a breakup in my current, vulnerable state of recovery seemed like trying to swim against a powerful current.

Note to Self:
Actions speak
louder than
words.

So, I did my usual "dance." I pushed down my emotional pain and immersed myself in work, using it as a distraction to escape my personal life. I popped some over-the-counter pain pills and embarked on my forty-five-minute commute. The stitches pulled at my skin, almost threatening to burst open with every movement, but I refused to give in to the pain. I pushed through it, determined to prove my resilience. Plus, the thought of returning to my apartment only added to my determination to tough it out. At work, I put on a brave face. I didn't want to make a fuss or draw attention to myself. I longed for everything to return to normal, although I wasn't sure what 'normal' meant anymore.

During the workday, my coworker Miles came over to chat. He greeted me cheerfully, saying, "Hey there, Amber!"

He doled out an enthusiastic high-five. In an attempt to meet his enthusiasm, I moved swiftly to return the gesture. However, as I did so, a sharp pain shot through my abdomen - clearly, that was a mistake. Miles noticed my wince.

"You alright?" he asked with concern in his voice.

"Not really," I admitted. "I'm still healing from having my gallbladder and appendix removed, and it's been tough."

"Two surgeries!? I had no idea," he admitted.

How could he not know? Then, it dawned on me that despite being in the hospital twice, my work continued to get done from my bed. It wasn't like I was broadcasting my surgeries to the whole staff, but I'd hoped the company would be worried about me or at least realize I was gone.

"You know, my sister got her gallbladder removed, and it was the best thing she ever did," Miles noted, trying to break the awkward silence between us.

While probably well-intentioned, his words fell flat. It was as if he didn't fully grasp the extent of my pain or how to relate. But it wasn't his fault. Remote work made it easy to assume people were working from home if they weren't in the office.

"I probably should have taken the day off or worked from home, but I didn't want to be cooped up any longer," I said, thinking aloud.

"Well, take care of yourself and go home early if you need to," he said. "If you need anything, just holler."

When work was over (yes, I stayed for my entire eight-hour shift), I hurried down the stairs to the subway station and squeezed into the packed car. It was rush hour, and no seats were available. Unfortunately, my internal pain wasn't visible enough to prompt anyone to offer me their seat.

To take my mind off the pain radiating from my healing body, I got lost in deep introspection. I found it funny that I started the day trying to escape my personal life, but by the end, I had an overwhelming desire to flee from my corporate grind, too. Pushing myself to endure the pain and make it into the office wouldn't earn me praise or promotions. In fact, if I wasn't careful, this kind of stress and disregard for my well-being could land me back in the hospital again.

It was clear that something needed to change, and soon. I wasn't content, let alone happy. I wondered if it was time to adopt a Marie Kondo approach to my life - letting go of anything that no longer sparked joy.

I sent a silent plea to the universe, asking for a sign. When I lifted my gaze, the answer was right there emblazed on a colorful advertisement: **"It's now or never."**

PART TWO

Permission to Blow Up My Life in 3, 2, 1

CHAPTER EIGHT

The Great Resignation

"I want to blow up my life," I blurted to my best friend, Heidi. As the words spilled from my lips, I felt a sudden release like a thousand-pound weight was off my shoulders. These thoughts had been swirling in my mind for months, but this was the first time I had let them out into the world. Heidi wasn't entirely shocked by my revelation. She was the one person who was privy to the details of my work and relationship struggles. Still, the scale of what I was proposing gave her pause.

"What do you mean exactly?" she asked.

"I want to leave it all behind - quit my job, call off my engagement, leave New York City, and move closer to my family," I admitted with a heavy sigh.

"Slow down," Heidi said.

"I'm not happy anymore," I replied, slumping onto the couch and running a hand through my hair.

"You're not joking, are you?" she asked.

"I wish I was," I responded, shaking my head. "But everything is suffocating me. The job is draining, the city is chaotic, and my engagement feels more like a black hole sucking the life out of me than a relationship."

The last confession stung.

Heidi listened and was a picture of patience and understanding, occasionally sipping her sparkling rose.

"Take a hard look at your finances," she advised, her tone taking on a serious note that I knew to pay attention to. "Figure out how long you can sustain yourself with what you've saved. Money is not everything, but it is important when you're considering such a big life change."

It made sense. Years of faithfully saving now provided me with a financial cushion. And although an early withdrawal might come with a tax penalty, it seemed a small price to pay for the precious freedom it would afford.

"I've taken countless leaps of faith in my life without any guarantee of success, and I'm doing just fine," I declared.

I truly believed the universe would weave its magic and everything would work out.

"If your gut still says this is what you need, go for it. Always trust your instinct; it knows you better than anyone else ever will," Heidi assured me.

"I've always embodied the 'go big or go home' mentality," I laughed.

"And that's why we're friends," Heidi smiled.

"I'm going to do it," I said. "First up, I'm quitting my job."

* * *

"Showtime!" I yelled while on my morning commute to work.

Suddenly, the bustling subway car transformed into a grand stage. I leaped onto the seats, striking a powerful pose, as fellow passengers-turned-backup dancers cheered me on. The fierce anthem of Christina Aguilera's "Fighter" blared through the subway car.

With each beat, my confidence grew. I swung around the poles, my eyes filled with determination and spirit. Then came my signature move to mark the finale: I did a spinning jump into a perfect split.

"Amber! Amber! Amber!" the fellow New Yorkers roared.

I reveled in the applause.

But the sudden lurch of the subway snapped me out of my daydream, grounding me back into reality. I found myself amidst a sea of commuters, each ensnared in their own universe of thoughts.

"Stand clear of the closing doors, please," the voice bellowed over the train's speakers.

My whimsical fantasy served as a delightful interlude to the day ahead; I was about the put in my two-week notice at work, and I didn't have another job lined up.

Despite the risks, I knew that quitting my job needed to be the initial spark to ignite the cascade of transformations I was planning. Holding onto that realization, I made my way into the office.

My impending decision to quit rendered me unable to concentrate effectively. I found myself aimlessly shuffling papers on my desk and mindlessly scrolling through my inbox. Caught in a cycle of trying to find the perfect moment to deliver my news yet continually delaying it, I became consumed with what to do next. So, I turned to an old habit - seeking refuge in the bathroom, a sanctuary I had relied on throughout my life when I needed to escape the company of others and regroup.

I ran through all the reasons that had brought me here: the grind, stalled growth, and my need for freedom away from NYC. Each one served as a reminder of why this was the right decision. Internally, I affirmed, *This decision is for my happiness and for a life that ignites joy and satisfaction. I have grown beyond this role, and it's time to make room for what comes next.*

I moved toward the mirror, positioning myself squarely in front of it. I straightened my posture, squaring my shoulders and lifting my chin slightly, adopting a power pose that radiated confidence and determination. The act gave me a sense of invincibility as if I was channeling some hidden superwoman from deep within me. After a few seconds, I let my arms drop.

I was ready.

It was now or never.

Back at my desk, I opened the internal work messaging platform and pinged my boss, "Hi, do you have a moment to chat?"

My screen lit up. "Sure, Amber, let's meet in the large conference room."

With a deep breath, I walked toward the room. I realized that I was not only quitting my job but also leaving behind colleagues who had become friends, routines that had provided a semblance of stability, and a salary to which I had become accustomed.

Once seated, we shared a few pleasantries, but my boss knew what was coming.

"I'm putting in my two-week notice," I said.

A weight lifted off my shoulders.

"Amber, is there anything we can do to make you reconsider?" she asked, rattling off a few incentives to sway my decision.

The company's sudden eagerness to offer more than my previous requests was flattering and downright annoying. Why does a person have to quit to finally be heard and offered the money they deserve?

"Thank you for the offer, but my decision is final," I replied firmly.

I understood from past experiences that when a workplace becomes so unbearable that it drives you to explore other options or quit, any additional money will only act as a temporary bandaid. You'll eventually quit again (*awkward!*), or the company will have your name at the top of the list when layoffs roll around.

My boss inquired about my future plans. I held my cards close, not divulging any details. The truth was, I needed a clean break and didn't want anything to tie me down to the city.

So with a mischievous smile, I played coy, "You'll find out soon enough."

* * *

As I pushed open our apartment door, the warm scent of home-cooked food and soft music greeted me.

Then came Luke, who enveloped me in his arms. He brushed my hair away from my face, and our lips met in a gentle and intoxicating kiss. As we pulled apart, Luke led me to the couch, a familiar place where we had shared countless evenings.

"Amber, you're a bad*ss," he began, his eyes shining with admiration. "You're so brave for quitting your job. Do you know how many people talk about doing that but who don't have the guts to do so?"

His words calmed my nerves, and for a brief moment, I felt so connected with him.

Taking in the careful preparation, the mood-setting, and the praise, I smiled.

"Did you go through all this trouble for me?" I inquired, genuinely touched by the apparent effort.

He nodded.

We engaged in lighthearted conversation, discussing the events of our respective days. Yet, the illusion of celebration gradually crumbled as I began to perceive the underlying truth behind these seemingly heartfelt gestures.

"Oh, by the way, I should've told you sooner," Luke began, staring directly into my eyes, "but tomorrow, I'm spending the day with Crystal."

I felt my stomach churn.

He continued, "She's treating me to a belated birthday lunch."

Heat rose in my cheeks. The thought of them dining at some fancy restaurant while I was at home, jobless and alone, was infuriating.

"Of all the times you could've chosen to spend the day with her, why now?" I asked.

But I knew why.

Luke had been passive-aggressive with me since his birthday celebration plans fell through a few weeks prior. I had meticulously organized an intimate sushi dinner at one of the trendiest spots in the city, reserving the entire counter for him and a handful of his closest friends.

However, life threw a curveball when a new COVID-19 variant hit the city. Concerned for their safety, his friends made the tough choice to bow out, and I couldn't blame them. Health and safety had to come first. But to Luke, it felt like a personal attack. He couldn't see past his disappointment, and I found myself the unfortunate target of his fury. His words cut deep, accusing me of purposely ruining his special day.

A part of me wanted to reschedule the party, but his spiteful reaction stopped me. What was the point of trying if nothing I did was good enough for him?

In what felt like a vindictive move, Luke accepted Crystal's offer to treat him to a belated birthday lunch. They would be dining at an upscale restaurant while I sat home, uninvited. If he intended to rub salt into the wound, he succeeded.

To add insult to injury, he casually gave me a rundown of their agenda. After the lavish lunch at a Michelin-star restaurant, they intended to have drinks and head to the Edge, the famous observation deck at Hudson Yards that offered breathtaking city views from a dizzying hundred stories high. The mention of the Edge was a slap in the face. It had been the spot we had gone to for a date to mend our relationship after he initially confessed his confusing feelings for Crystal.

I felt a rage simmering inside me.

"I'm not okay with how close you two are," I shot back, unable to mask the venom in my tone, "but you do you."

Luke, however, seemed unperturbed.

"Crystal got a new job and is leaving the city in two weeks. We want to hang out before the big move," he countered, trying to justify his plans.

"And, by the way, she is taking me out," he added, emphasizing those words unnecessarily, "not the other way around."

Whether he was blind to my feelings or didn't care, I couldn't tell, but either way, his lack of consideration felt like a betrayal. I was seething, angry at not only Luke but at myself for not setting more explicit boundaries earlier in our relationship. I lost myself because I wanted to be loved.

"Fine, go. Enjoy yourself," I muttered, forcing a smile onto my face even as my heart splintered into a thousand broken pieces.

"Amber, after tomorrow, she's pretty much out of my life because she's moving away from the city," he said.

"I just don't get why you need to hang out without me," I replied.

"Well, do you want to come?" he asked.

"Honestly, no," I scoffed.

"Then, why are you making a big deal about it? Crystal and I are just going to be talking about work anyway. You'll be so bored," he told me.

My inner warrior had been knocked out. I no longer had the strength to argue about his friendships with other women. The constant accusations of jealousy left me feeling worn out, unheard, and overwhelmingly tired.

When the next day rolled around, Luke meticulously got ready, looking extra sharp and presentable. He spritzed on his favorite cologne, the scent lingering in the air as he stepped out of the bathroom. Every hair combed to perfection.

As he walked out, he kissed me goodbye.

Luke, oblivious to the seismic shift growing in my heart, walked out the door. At that moment, I was done tolerating his behavior. It was time for me to reclaim my life, stand up for myself, and demand the respect and love I deserved. Luke was about to discover a new version of me who wouldn't settle for feeling unsafe or unheard. I was over it, and more importantly, I was over him.

Note to Self:
Some things break
your heart but fix
your vision.

CHAPTER NINE

The Time-Out Tango

Startled by the sound of my name echoing through the apartment, I froze in the shower, naked and vulnerable. I cautiously pulled back the shower curtain, only to come face to face with an unexpected sight: Luke had brought Crystal upstairs.

In an attempt to address the elephant in the room, Luke ventured, "Amber, I thought you might like to meet Crystal. I hoped it would help alleviate any feelings of jealousy or resentment."

I took a moment to gather my thoughts.

With a mixture of curiosity and apprehension, I replied, "I appreciate the gesture, but can you give me a minute?"

I hastily threw on some clothes and disregarded any thought of makeup. Gathering my composure as best as possible, I made my way to the kitchen where Crystal and Luke stood, waiting. The air was charged with unease as we faced each other.

"It's too bad you didn't come with us today. You would have loved it," Crystal said.

Her words caught me off guard. I glanced at Luke; my confusion was evident in my gaze.

"Oh, I didn't think I was invited," I replied.

As if to defuse the awkwardness, Luke pulled out a photo, attempting to divert the conversation. It was a photo he and Crystal had taken atop The Edge.

I mustered a laugh and retrieved the very same photo he and I had once captured during our own visit. Awkwardness loomed in the air. Sensing the tension, Crystal excused herself, saying she needed to get home to let her dog out.

We shared a brief, genuine hug because I had no animosity toward her. My frustration was squarely with Luke.

Luke offered to walk Crystal to her car, leaving me alone in the apartment once more.

When he returned, a hint of excitement laced his words. "Isn't she awesome?"

The weight of my mounting frustration finally gave, and I dropped the bombshell on Luke.

"I can't do this anymore. This relationship has taken its toll on me, and I think we need to break up," I asserted.

Luke, taken aback by the proposal, pleaded with a hint of desperation, "Amber, you don't truly mean that, do you?"

"I do," I said.

Despite my readiness to walk away, Luke proposed we go to couples therapy. His plea for one last attempt at salvaging our relationship tugged at my heartstrings. I gave in to him... again.

Tasked with finding a suitable therapist, I scoured the Internet. After carefully considering my options and reading numerous online reviews, I selected Dr. V, a couple's therapist who seemed suitable for our needs. With a sense of cautious optimism, I scheduled our first session.

Luke expressed his trust in my judgment, assuring me that he didn't need to vet the therapist before our first session. He placed his confidence in me, understanding that I had carefully considered our options.

A few days later, we hopped onto a virtual Zoom call, about to meet our therapist for the first time. As we embarked on this vital step toward seeking professional guidance and support, nervous anticipation filled the air.

As we dove into what brought us to couple's therapy, Dr. V asked us to recount how we fell in love - those early days marked by laughter and shared dreams. There had been an undeniable spark that drew us together like magnets.

We spoke of all the things that made us fall in love. Luke bragged about my passion for life, creative talents, and loyalty. I gushed about his humor, how great a cook and host he was for our friends, and how I loved watching him in his element, effortlessly navigating the intricacies of the legal system with an unwavering dedication to his clients.

As the session progressed, the mention of Crystal's name caused an undeniable shift in the air. I could feel my grip tightening on the armrest, a physical manifestation of the discomfort that enveloped us.

With sensitivity, our therapist gently probed if there were any past traumas or unresolved baggage that I had brought into our partnership, recognizing the potential impact on our dynamics. Without missing a beat, Luke transitioned to a sensitive chapter from my past.

"Amber had an experience with an ex-boyfriend who cheated on her," he stated. "I believe that might be affecting her trust in me, though I've given her no reason to question my loyalty."

Of course, my past experiences had left scars, but I couldn't believe Luke was conveniently using my past against me, painting me as the one with trust issues. It was a clever tactic, a deflection from his actions to make me the crazy one who needed to "fix" herself.

I began to share fragments of my personal history, the moments of heartbreak, cheating, and betrayal that had left lingering imprints on my trust and sense of security.

Our therapist listened attentively, offering empathetic nods and gentle reassurances as I described crossed boundaries and our lack of communication.

"I'm trying, Amber," Luke interjected, his tone pleading as he turned toward me in our therapy session.

"But the thing is, I've been asking for change for nearly a year. I don't think talking about it is enough anymore. I need to see real change," I said.

I could feel the therapist's eyes flitting between us, observing our exchange like a spectator at a tennis match. I couldn't shake off the feeling that we were spinning our wheels, going around in circles without making any real progress.

As our session continued, Luke assumed a familiar role, taking command of the conversation. His natural charisma filled the room. His voice was calm and composed, laced with the charm he was so known for. He explained how, yes, he had many close female friends, but they didn't in any way jeopardize his commitment to me.

The therapist, seemingly enamored by his convincing narrative, nodded along. His tales were winning her over, as they had won over so many others.

"Luke, it seems like you're really trying," she commented, affirming his perspective and leaving me feeling invalidated.

I found myself questioning if I was overreacting. The session was supposed to be about us, but I felt like I was the one on trial, with Luke as the eloquent attorney and the therapist as the captivated jury.

My confusion only intensified when the therapist weaved a personal story into our narrative, saying she'd been in my shoes before. She revealed that her ex-husband cheated on her and that she projected her past hurt onto her new boyfriend and had to undertake a personal journey of healing and growth to overcome that.

"My insecurities and walls nearly tore our relationship apart, but now, we've been blissfully together for a decade," she said.

I was baffled. Why was her story being imposed on our session? Was it customary for a therapist to share such intimate details in a session that we were footing the bill for?

I finally decided to speak up.

"Okay, Crystal isn't the only thing going wrong here," I admitted.

I launched into how Luke and I also disagreed about the most basic things -- like a roll of toilet paper.

* * *

My intention, I thought, was clear: I wanted to lighten Luke's load and provide him with a well-deserved moment of relaxation. So I went to the store and got our food and necessities for the week.

Luke, however, was not happy about it.

"You bought the wrong toilet paper!" he lashed out.

"I was just trying to help," I tried to explain, somewhat blindsided.

"I was going to go to the store while you were out with your friends at the Steelers bar, but I guess that isn't happening now," he said with a huff.

His words hit me like a punch to the gut. I was already in my Steelers jersey, ready to watch the game, but I felt so guilty now, like I'd ruined his whole day.

"Do you want me to go get the right toilet paper? Or stay here with you instead?" I asked.

"No, just go," Luke replied.

So I did.

Anger and frustration consumed every ounce of my body. I felt unhinged and couldn't help but feel trapped in a catch-22 situation—damned if I do, damned if I don't.

When I got to the bar, I was ready for a drink. And before I knew it, a solitary Tito's and soda multiplied into a trio. Not stopping there, I called for a bottle of bubbly to grace our table. Yeah, the Steelers were losing, but I needed the extra liquid courage. I wanted to tell my friends about my latest tiff with Luke, and it wasn't an easy chat. For most of our relationship, I kept his behavior tucked away, shielded from public scrutiny. I didn't want to air our dirty laundry and strived to maintain this ideal image of us.

But now, with the alcohol acting as an emotional lubricant, I spilled the details of our recent argument, including the baffling focus on that ludicrous toilet paper episode.

My friends tuned into my every word. Their faces morphed from a show of worry to one of sheer disbelief.

"He's mad about toilet paper?! That's not normal," my friend Hailey said, shaking her head in disbelief.

My other friends nodded in unison.

"That seems like an odd thing to argue about when you're engaged to be married. Maybe it's not about toilet paper? Is he stressed out at work? Is he getting cold feet? That behavior seems out of character for him," my other friend Blake noted.

"I just don't know," I said, tears filling my eyes. "I'm so frustrated and scared to think this will be the rest of my life if I marry him."

Note to Self:
You're not selfish
for wanting to be
treated well.

As the afternoon progressed, I knew if I went home even a little drunk, I'd subject myself to another explosive argument with Luke about my drinking.

"Can I sleep this off at your place?" I asked Hailey.

"Yes, we got you, Amber," she replied.

Understanding the gravity of the situation, I told her to call Luke and let him know crashed at her place. I hoped it would mitigate any further escalation. Once again, I was wrong.

When my tired eyes fluttered open, I glanced at the clock and gasped. It was 5 a.m.

I had unintentionally spent the entire night on Hailey's couch. This was not how I wanted things to unfold. In a frantic rush, I gathered my belongings and got an Uber to take me home. The realization of my prolonged absence hit me. How would Luke react? I was terrified to find out.

As I walked into the apartment, Luke's disapproving gaze met mine.

"I was worried sick about you. You didn't even text me to let me know you were coming home. I feared for your safety," he said.

Guilt washed over me as I tried to explain, "I'm sorry, Luke. I didn't mean to worry you. I completely passed out on the couch. It was never my intention to stay overnight. And yes, I should have texted you to tell you I was coming home safely."

He huffed and scolded me. At that moment, I felt like that little girl in church who was supposed to be a good girl, stay quiet, and play small. I'd been disobedient, and now my future husband was angry.

Coming back to reality, I stood there, scared.

"Luke," I began, trembling, "I'm sorry. My decision to go out, drink, and not come home was irresponsible and disrespectful. I hadn't planned on staying through the night, but it happened."

I desperately hoped that he would understand and see my remorse and determination to make things right.

"But there's something else I need to address," I continued, feeling a knot of anxiety tightening in my stomach. "The toilet paper incident. It might seem insignificant in the grand scheme, but it is about how we communicate and handle our disagreements."

"We do need to communicate better. But it felt like you disregarded my preferences when you got the wrong toilet paper. I felt you did it intentionally as if you weren't considering my feelings," he paused, swallowing hard before continuing, his tone growing stronger with every word. "I felt unheard and overlooked. As if my opinions, even about the smallest of things, didn't matter to you."

His next words hit me like a punch to the gut.

"And why would you go shopping without me when you know it's one of my favorite things?"

Shopping was our thing, a tradition, a shared experience that we both cherished.

"I understand," I said, "but I was only trying to help lighten your load and give you one less thing to think about this weekend. You've been working so much lately."

The conversation was over, its conclusion far from satisfying.

Later that evening, we reconvened.

"You hungry?" he asked.

"Yes, what are you thinking?" I asked.

"Ugh, just decide and pick something," he said.

"Okay.... let's order tacos," I said.

He was clearly disappointed by my choice.

"How about pizza?" he nudged.

"Okay. Pizza it is," I said.

"Well, don't just say pizza because I want it," he retorted.

Damned if I do, damned if I don't.

We ordered pizza.

* * *

As the session wrapped, the therapist suggested that Luke and I take a two-week break.

"But won't that just drive us further apart?" I asked.

"This is a chance for both of you to clear your heads. It's about creating space for growth for individual reflection. This distance might actually bring you closer together in the long run," she continued.

"Let's try it," Luke said.

"He's giving you a gift, Amber," the therapist said with a smile.

It sure didn't seem like a gift, but I felt like I had to go along with the plan to say I tried.

"Alright," I said, "I'm in."

We decided to set ground rules and clarified, first and foremost, that this wasn't a breakup.

"We're not pulling a Ross and Rachel," I said, trying to inject some humor into the tense atmosphere.

Luke chuckled at the *Friends* reference.

"We're on a break, but not that kind of break," I added.

"Yes, and no contact," Luke stated.

I nodded in agreement. The idea was to have complete separation and live independently for those two weeks - no calls, texts, or social media check-ins. It would be difficult, but we both knew it was necessary.

Because Luke's job required him to stay in the city, it made sense for him to stay in the apartment. I agreed to take this opportunity to visit my family again in Ohio.

* * *

Back in Ohio, I stood in front of the mirror, staring into the eyes of a stranger. The confident, radiant woman who used to stare back was now just a distant memory, her effervescence muted by the years of self-diminishing compromise.

My reflection seemed to ask, "How did we end up here?"

My heart echoed with regret. I had lost precious time and dimmed my own light, all in the pursuit of trying to be chosen by a man. Luke had been my entire universe, but in making him so, I had lost sight of my worth. I had lived in denial for too long, accepting these breadcrumbs as signs of love. But this was not the woman I wanted to be. I was deserving of a love that was respectful, attentive, and reciprocal. My self-worth was not contingent on Luke's validation but was an inherent quality that I needed to embrace.

The love I felt for him, intense as it was, was not a compelling enough reason to remain in a relationship that was steadily eroding my self-esteem and emotional well-being. I needed to free myself from the harmful patterns of our relationship, even if it meant letting Luke go. I needed to finally hold him accountable.

I began to realize the love I had so desperately sought from others—validation, acceptance, the desire to be seen and cherished—was already within me. I didn't need anyone else to make me feel worthy or valued. I was enough, just as I was.

As the couple's therapist aptly put it, the distance from Luke was a blessing in disguise. I could finally see that walking away would be not only an act of self-preservation but an act of self-love.

*   *   *

The kitchen was calm; the only sound punctuating the silence was the low drone of the refrigerator. Sitting around the wooden table, I called a family meeting, finally finding the courage to open up to my parents. It was day five of Luke and I's separation.

"Mom, Dad," I began, "I need to leave Luke and move out of our apartment."

My father's eyes met mine, filled with both concern and resolve. He quickly proposed a plan of action and offered me a much-needed lifeline.

"I'll rent a U-Haul, drive to New York, and pack up your things," he said. "How soon do you want me to get there?"

I was in awe. My father was ready to embark on an 18-hour roundtrip journey to help me. The gesture was not lost on me. This selfless gesture highlighted the lengths he would go to for me. In the past, I often found it challenging to ask for help, trapped by my insecurities and fear of asking for "too much." But when I looked at my parents, we all shared an unspoken agreement: My dad was renting the U-Haul.

Note to Self:
Be humble enough
to know when to
ask for help.

* * *

My phone began to ring, lighting up with an unknown number. Ordinarily, I'd have just let it go to voicemail - I wasn't a fan of picking up calls from numbers I didn't recognize. But something in my gut nudged me to answer it this time. So, I swiped the screen and brought the phone to my ear.

"Hello?" I answered the call.

To my surprise, it was a recruiter calling about a communications job I applied for at a prominent national healthcare organization. I submitted my application months ago, so the opportunity had been off my radar. Still, I tried to stay cool.

"Thank you for getting back to me," I told the recruiter.

"We were quite impressed with your resume and felt you could be a good fit for the role. Are you still interested?"

"Absolutely, I'm very interested," I responded enthusiastically. "This call is actually a pleasant surprise."

"That's great to hear! Our team would like to set up an interview with you to learn more about your qualifications and discuss the role in further detail," the recruiter informed me.

Long story short, after a round of interviews, I landed the job - all during my two-week break from Luke. What are the chances?

"We're confident you're the perfect fit for this role," the recruiter told me over the phone.

It's interesting how life unfolds and how this new job opportunity only appeared after I had let go of my previous one. It's like life was reminding me that sometimes we need to release things that no longer benefit us to make room for growth and fresh starts.

Obtaining a role in the public health sector provided an opportunity to make a positive difference in people's lives. Plus, my personal health challenges from the previous year only made me even more determined to be of service to others and felt like an opportunity to "pay it forward."

Despite my impulse to reach out to Luke, who had been my rock and confidant for years, I knew that calling him during our agreed-upon "no contact" period would only hinder my healing process and make things more difficult in the long run. So, I ran downstairs to tell my mom the news.

"Mom, I got the job!" I exclaimed.

"Congratulations," she said, giving me a big hug. "Let's drink to that."

It was the first time in years we could celebrate the joy of a new job offer together in real time. As we clinked our wine glasses together, I couldn't believe everything had aligned so perfectly. I soaked up every bit of this joyous moment, knowing the days ahead would be dark and challenging; breaking up with Luke wouldn't be easy.

CHAPTER TEN

Breaking (the) News

Confronting conflict head-on had never been my strong suit. I'd grown up not wanting to "rock the boat," so I preferred peaceful discussions to heated arguments because it came more easily to me.

The thought of facing Luke and breaking up brought a sense of impending dread. What scared me the most was not the act of ending our engagement but the aftermath - his reaction and the prospect of sharing the same space with him after delivering the news.

My mind played out every possible scenario, both good and bad. However, there was a particular fear that clung to me. I was afraid that Luke's anger, a side of him I had unfortunately witnessed before, might erupt. I had to mentally prepare myself for whatever was coming.

"I'm so scared to go back to New York," I admitted to my parents. "I wish I could send someone else to pack my things and break up with Luke."

Deep down, I knew that wasn't an option. I owed him the courtesy of breaking up in person. It was the right thing to do. I kept reminding myself that I only needed to navigate forty-eight hours by myself before my parents arrived together in a U-Haul to help me pack up my life.

I can do it, I repeated over and over.

"Do you think he'll hurt you?" they asked.

"Physically? I don't think so, but breakups can make people do crazy sh*t," I said.

"Promise me something," I continued. "No matter what I say in the next two days, like if I tell you to turn back, don't listen to me. Come anyway because I might not be strong enough to do this alone."

I explained that Luke might try to convince me to stay, or I might get scared and change my mind about this whole plan.

My mom and dad understood.

With our plans set, I embraced my parents tightly before heading toward the airport terminal. Tears welled in my eyes, blurring the sight of my parents, their faces etched with concern and love. The weight of the situation and the uncertainty of what was to come made the moment even more poignant. The next few days would probably be some of the toughest I'd face; I just hoped I'd make it to the other side of the breakup.

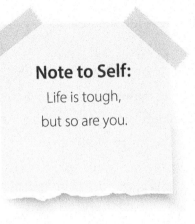

Note to Self:
Life is tough,
but so are you.

* * *

I stood outside our apartment door, frozen for a few minutes as I gathered the courage to walk in. I wondered what awaited me on the other side. Finally, I let out a deep sigh before inserting my keys into the lock. My stomach churned as I braced myself for what was to come. With a twist and a push, I stepped over the threshold, holding my breath. The familiar smell of Luke's woody cologne hit me as I walked into the apartment. He came bouncing to the door like a puppy dog.

A superficial smile was etched on my face as I endured his embrace. Every nerve within me was on high alert.

As we pulled apart, Luke stared deep into my eyes.

"Amber, these two weeks apart from you have made me realize something," he said.

I felt my heart tighten, bracing myself for the wave of anger his words would unleash.

"I don't want to be without you, Amber. It felt like a piece of me was missing while you were gone," he said.

His earnest confession hung in the air. I swallowed hard, mustering up the courage to reply.

"Luke," I started, my voice shaky, "these two weeks have been... different for me."

"Amber, we've had our ups and downs, but we can get through this. Relationships take work, and I hate to bail when we've built something so beautiful," he said.

I shook my head, which led Luke to spiral into a plea of desperation.

"I know I told you I wasn't a big fan of marriage and that it's just a piece of paper, but we can get married tomorrow at the courthouse if that's what you want. I want to spend the rest of my life with you."

"And I'll never talk to Crystal again," he added to his long list of promises.

It was hard to believe that he suddenly wanted to change. He had countless chances, so this renewed vow, regardless of its sincerity, seemed more like a manipulation to me—a desperate scheme designed to drag me back into the toxic cycle.

Going into this conversation, I hoped the breakup would be mutual; this, I felt, would make the situation less painful.

The buildup to the breakup felt like a ticking time bomb. Each passing second was loaded with anxiety and every word had to be handled with delicate care.

It was now or never.

"Luke, I've been thinking a lot over the past two weeks, and I think we're better apart."

"What... what are you saying, Amber?" he stuttered.

"I love you, Luke, but we're not good for each other anymore. I think it's best if we break up," I said.

I could see him beginning to comprehend the gravity of what I was saying. I was done playing games. If I couldn't handle his close relationship with women like Crystal, I needed to step aside and walk away.

"Amber, please," he pleaded, reaching for my hands. "We can work this out. I promise I'll change. I'll cut off these friendships, and, as I said, I'll never talk to Crystal again. I'll do whatever it takes. Please, don't leave me."

"I can't keep going in circles with you," I said. "I want to let you go, so you can find a woman who is a better fit for you and that you don't want to change."

Suddenly, his pleas for reconsideration became more desperate as he tried to convince me that we could live happily ever after.

The next forty-eight hours unfolded like a whirlwind of messy emotions and heightened tension. Luke oscillated between tearful apologies to bouts of anger.

He erupted when I told him my parents were already en route to our place, and my decision to break up was final.

"What is this... a damn rescue mission?" he said.

His questions came at me relentlessly, rendering me feeling cornered and powerless. Seated on the couch, I suddenly felt like a criminal in an interrogation room. Each question seemed intended to wear me down and break me.

"Why now, after all we've been through together?"

"Haven't I been a good partner to you? Haven't I tried my best?"

"So, you're just going to walk away? Just like that, without even trying to fix things?"

The man I had loved for years was now a stranger, and I didn't know how to escape this situation. Luke wasn't going to make it easy for me.

* * *

The sudden da-da-dah of my iPhone's ringtone jolted me awake. Disoriented and groggy, I looked at the screen and saw two words from my mom: "We're here."

How long had Luke and I been going around in circles about our relationship? When did I fall asleep? What day was it?

As I made my way to the door to let my parents into the building, I realized Luke wouldn't let me leave without a fight. The room seemed to shrink, the air growing dense with tension. I had made my intentions clear; our relationship was over, but Luke refused to accept it.

Luke stood firm, stubbornly obstructing the door that symbolized my freedom.

"Don't leave," he begged. "Let's keep talking."

"Please let me go," I pleaded, but he wouldn't budge. "My parents are waiting outside. Let's not draw this out any longer."

"No!" he said, barricading himself between me and the apartment door.

There had never been any physical violence in our relationship, but at this moment, my body shook with primal and raw terror. Would I make it out alive? I didn't know.

My parents were so near, yet so achingly far. I silently wished they'd knock down the door and rescue me. But they found themselves helplessly marooned outside. I painstakingly attempted to negotiate my exit from the apartment. It was a delicate dance.

Many details about what transpired over the sixty minutes have vanished into oblivion as if I was in a disorienting blackout. What I do remember though is writing Crystal's name on a piece of paper and lighting it on fire. (Luke's idea.) The orange and red flames devoured the innocent parchment. It wasn't a petty act of vengeance but rather an attempt to sage her away. As the paper burned to ashes, I looked down at my hand. There, on my finger, was my engagement ring - a beautiful, tangible symbol of a once-promised future. The diamond sparkled under the flames.

With a heavy heart, I slid the ring off my finger. The cold metal felt unnaturally heavy, and sorrow surged within me. Unrestrained, heart-wrenching sobs shook my entire body. As the tears flowed and the ring lay cold in my hand, the finality of our separation became real. It was a moment of profound pain and loss.

"So, this is really it?" Luke asked. He seemed to be searching for anything that might indicate a possibility of reconciliation.

"Yes," I replied.

Our story had reached its end, and as much as it hurt, it was time to turn the page. Luke popped a bottle of champagne and started drinking straight from the bottle. After a few swigs, and one last-ditch attempt to persuade me to reconsider, he surrendered.

Luke finally gave in to my pleas and offered to walk me downstairs, a silent admission that our standoff was ending. He drew me into a final embrace.

"I love you, Amber James. I always will," he said.

As he let go, we both knew this was our final goodbye. It was the end of us, our shared history, and our future together.

His brow creased, hands in his pockets. He looked different. Vulnerable, almost.

"I can't be here. It's just...it's too hard. I don't want to watch you pack up your life. I have to leave," his voice choked.

"I understand," I nodded.

With a final glance at me, he said, "I hope you find what you're looking for," his voice quivered.

"Thank you," I whispered.

Note to Self:
Prioritize
happiness
over history.

As Luke's footsteps grew fainter, I made a beeline for the loading dock, hoping to find my parents.

The sight of them, patiently standing by the U-Haul truck, washed over me like a tidal wave. I burst into tears.

"I love you," I managed to choke out through my sobs.

My mom and dad both hugged me tightly.

"It's going to be okay," they said.

And with that, the three of us got to work.

We haphazardly gathered my belongings over the next three hours and boxed up my life. It was overwhelming, and I underestimated the sheer volume of it all. Every drawer

I opened, and every closet I emptied seemed to hold more than I remembered.

My dad and I glanced nervously at the U-Haul truck, its vast emptiness soon to be filled. We shared a brief, anxious laugh, the tension momentarily broken.

"Do you think we can fit all this in there?" he asked, his voice laced with humor but his eyes hinting at genuine concern.

"I sure hope so," I responded, forcing a smile onto my face.

With each box packed, I tried to maintain a brave face and focus on the end goal. Occasionally, I would halt, allowing waves of sadness to engulf me. The grief was intricate, a layered web of shame for the relationship I stayed in too long and the life I was leaving behind in New York City.

As the last of my items were placed into a tote, I recorded a two-minute video capturing my final moments in the apartment.

"I am so incredibly sad," I whimpered. "My New York story shouldn't have ended this way, but it did. And now I am standing here in this apartment, and there's no piece of me left."

The video panned across the living room, revealing empty shelves. Seeing it devoid of my trinkets, paintings, and pictures that once made it my home was strange. I gasped for air, on the verge of hyperventilating, and buried my face in my dark green Ohio University hoodie. My eyes were red and swollen.

"Why Luke? Why?!" I cried into the camera before crumbling onto the floor.

Even though I'd been the one to end the relationship, I was shattered. I wished so deeply that Luke would have done something - anything - to put our relationship before his desire to have all these female friends. It didn't have to end this way. But it did.

Taking a deep breath, I walked around the empty apartment one last time.

"I think that's everything. Let's go," I said.

My mom and dad came up behind me, wrapping me in their arms. As I leaned into their love, I realized how much time I had spent trying not to bother others with my problems. It was like I had built a wall around myself, insisting on carrying my burdens alone. I understood that those who truly cared about me wanted to be there for me and help lighten my load, no matter how heavy or insignificant it may seem. They wanted to share not just the moments of joy but also the struggles, the tears, and the setbacks. It dawned on me that I did not have to face my struggles alone, and accepting help from those who cared about me was not a burden but a gift of love.

At 36, I was still their baby, a reality unaffected by time or events. My parents saw me not only as the grown woman I had become but also as the child whose scraped knees they had kissed, whose tears they had wiped, and whose dreams they had nurtured. To them, my age was irrelevant. I was forever their child, deserving of their protection and love, no matter what.

As we walked out of the apartment together, I took one last glance back.

"Goodbye," I whispered.

As I closed the door behind me, I realized this simple act was symbolic— it was also closing the chapter that Luke and I had written together. A new wave of tears trickled down my cheeks. It was over. My hand lingered on the door a moment longer, a silent farewell imprinted in the cool touch of the steel.

"Good luck, Luke," I murmured to myself.

Reflecting on my New York journey, I realized that my arrival and departure shared a common thread—taking a leap of faith. When I first moved to the city, I was somewhat naive, trusting everything would work out. I had arrived post-college with just two suitcases and a dream, and my parents helped me settle into my first apartment, a tiny Harlem guesthouse with a shared bathroom. I believed in my ability to carve a path for myself in the bustling metropolis. I did all that and so much more.

Now, I was embracing the same optimism - even through my sadness; I had faith that a new beautiful chapter awaited me, filled with opportunities and growth. I had survived living in New York City during the height of the pandemic, so I could survive the next adventure—wherever life took me.

I hopped into the U-Haul and hugged my parents.

"Thank you.. for everything," I said.

As we drove away, the sunset illuminated the city skyline, casting vibrant pinks and oranges over the city—a fitting symbol of the explosive change I'd ignited. In my wild imagination, with the city now to my back, I was like a phoenix rising from the ashes, fearlessly walking away from a blazing inferno, ready to start my reinvention.

Note to Self:
Goodbyes
allow for new
adventures.

PART THREE

Rising from the Ashes

CHAPTER ELEVEN

Three's Company

I quickly settled into my childhood home, which I nicknamed "The James Hotel." It was filled with warmth and numerous perks: home-cooked meals, laundry magically washed and folded, and the luxury of space and time to heal while surrounded by the people who knew me best.

Under different circumstances, the prospect of moving back in with my parents at thirty-six might have filled me with embarrassment. However, during this challenging life transition, I discovered a silver lining: I'd have the chance to make up for lost time with family. I loved every moment, and so did my parents.

Our days fell into a comfortable rhythm. In the mornings, my dad and I would sit in our pajamas, sipping hot coffee while watching episodes of the 1960s courtroom drama *Perry Mason.*

We debated the finer points of the cases and shared our theories, laughing at our amateur detective skills. My dad would point out the vintage cars featured on the show, filling me in on the details of each one. I cherished these moments of shared connection.

Mom and I developed a cherished afternoon ritual of taking leisurely walks around our neighborhood, chatting about everything and nothing at all until we reached "our tree."

Since I was a little girl, we created a quirky tradition of walking up to this majestic oak and tapping its trunk as if it gave us some magical powers. It may have seemed silly to outsiders, but it brought us immense joy.

And now, even though the landscape had changed, the tree still stood in all its glory. Its vast branches sprawled out like an inviting embrace against the sky, standing tall among the surrounding cornfields. As we got closer, my mom and I exchanged knowing smiles, reached out, and touched the rough, time-worn bark.

In these seemingly small moments, I realized how much I had missed this connection with my family. Having them nearby was essential to my healing, especially on the more challenging days, like when I bit into a Wendy's junior bacon cheeseburger and turned into a blubbering mess. The burger's sight, smell, and taste suddenly reminded me of

Luke because we stopped at this fast food chain on all our road trips to visit his family. My parents let me feel all the feelings - without judgment. It felt so good to cry.

Note to Self:
It's okay if all
you did today
was survive.

On another occasion, my niece asked, "When is Uncle Luke coming over to play superheroes with us again?"

She had no idea about the breakup. I hadn't disclosed the split to her because of her age. The question caught me off guard, and I felt a lump forming in my throat as I struggled to find the right words. How could I tell her the man who had once been a part of our lives was no longer a part of mine?

"I'm not sure," I replied, as my brain flashed back to when Luke came home with me. My nieces and nephew adored him, so it was devastating to think these moments were now just memories. He wouldn't be coming back to play superheroes.

I glanced at my mom, who was sitting nearby, and I whispered, "I need a moment."

I rushed upstairs to the sanctuary of my childhood bedroom. I found this space, which I had been so eager to leave decades prior, now offered a comforting refuge. I locked the door and collapsed onto my bed, allowing tears to stream down my face. It was a moment of raw vulnerability as I mourned the loss of my relationship with Luke again and the impact it would have on the people we both cared for.

After what felt like an eternity, my sobs began to subside, and I took in the sights of my childhood bedroom. My N'SYNC bobbleheads still stood on my dresser, making me giggle every time I saw their cartoonish faces bobbing.

I found my old AOL Instant Messenger handle scribbled on a piece of paper, serving as a delightful reminder of simpler times before Facebook and Instagram took over our lives. My diploma hung on the wall, symbolizing my accomplishments and the hard work I had put into my education.

And in the corner of the room stood my forest-green writing desk, adorned with the marks of pens, pencils, and markers – the battle scars of a young writer finding her voice. The sight of that desk brought back memories of countless hours spent writing.

Seeing that desk reminded me how far I'd come from the little girl who once dreamed of writing a book.

After that nostalgic journey through memory lane, I realized my tears had stopped. I was going to be okay.

I slowly made my way downstairs. When my mom saw me, she wrapped her arms around me, holding me close.

"It's okay to be sad," she whispered.

Each passing day became a little bit easier. The cloud of despair that had once crushed me began to lift, replaced by a growing light of hope and self-discovery. My eyes became less swollen and red, and I could finally sleep through the night. The tension that had once consumed my body slowly dissipated because I was no longer walking on eggshells or compromising my wants and needs for someone else. I was starting to feel like myself again and more in tune with who I was and who I wanted to be.

Living with my parents was a profoundly healing experience that made me realize there is no place like home.

CHAPTER TWELVE

No Turning Back

In the whirlwind of leaving NYC, I forgot to cancel Luke and I's upcoming therapy session. So, when the reminder unexpectedly flashed on my screen, it filled me with a sense of impending dread. The thought of facing Luke felt like a potential setback to my healing. However, I was also keenly aware that my absence might be interpreted as a lack of care or indifference, so I decided to log into the session.

As my computer connected to the therapy session, I heard Luke through the speakers.

"I'm not even sure if she's going to show up today," he confessed to the therapist. The subtext in his voice seemed carefully crafted to elicit sympathy, subtly positioning me as the villain in our shared story.

"Oh, I'm here," I declared.

Our therapist, accustomed to seeing us together, was visibly taken aback by our separate locations.

"I don't want to make any assumptions, so tell me, how did the two-week break go?"

There was no point in beating around the bush.

"Well, we've broken up, and I've already moved out," I said.

The therapist took a moment to digest the information.

"Oh, I'm sorry to hear that," she gently responded. "This must be a tough time for both of you."

Luke and I sat silent, so the therapist proposed a new direction for the session.

"I think it's important to give closure to this phase of our sessions," she suggested. "Would you both like to use this session to say whatever is on your minds or express anything left unsaid?"

Luke was the first to speak.

"I've written a letter. I want to read it now if that's okay," he said.

His words flowed, filled with expressions of regret, promises of change, and pleading for another chance. He admitted that he had taken me for granted and painted a picture of how different things would be if given a second chance.

It was heartbreaking to hear him pour out his soul. But even as he spoke of change, I couldn't help but remember the many times he had opportunities to change but chose not to.

His promises, though moving, were a painful reminder of a cycle I had finally broken free from. There was no turning back.

The therapist turned her gaze toward me. "Do you have anything to say?" she asked softly, giving me the space to articulate my feelings.

"Luke," I said, my voice calm and measured, "I appreciate your honesty, and I can see that you've given this a lot of thought. We've shared some beautiful moments, but we've also had our fair share of struggles. We tried but couldn't make it work despite our best efforts. Luke, you and I deserve to find happiness, even if it's not with each other."

The whole ordeal was a reminder that love alone wasn't always enough. Sometimes, you could love someone with every fiber of your being but know they were not right for you. So you have to let them go. In doing so, you honor not only your needs and well-being but theirs, too.

At the end of the session, which we agreed would be our last, Luke asked if he could still call me. I told him he could, even though I should have said, "No."

My phone rang, and it was Luke. Now with no therapist to play referee, he launched another effort to lure me back. His pleas were earnest, as if rehearsed to perfection, resonating with a desperate urgency. Luke tried his best to convince me of his intent to change. But actions speak louder than words, and I had no intention of getting back on this never-ending carousel of false promises and disappointments.

"Luke, you had so many chances to change. Why would I believe you now?" I asked.

As I attempted to end the call, he made one last desperate move, tossing out a Hail Mary in a final bid to win me back and gain my sympathy.

"Amber, this breakup... it's tearing me apart. I'm struggling. I want you to know that I contemplated jumping off our balcony yesterday," he confessed.

His words carried a heavy burden, leaving me torn. But this suicidal ideation seemed like a calculated ploy, designed to yank my emotional chains and reel me back into our toxic entanglement. It was simply too late for him now. I had to stand my ground.

"I want you to be safe, but I can't be the one to provide that support right now," I said. "I need time to heal, so Luke, please don't call me again."

Note to Self:
Self care is
not selfish.

CHAPTER THIRTEEN

It Takes a Village

Rebuilding my life wasn't easy and required a village of support (and a daily dose of Zoloft.) At times, it felt like I was assembling a ragtag team of superheroes, each with their own unique power to help me on my healing journey.

First up was my life coach, who had a knack for making me see things from a different perspective. Honestly, I used to be skeptical about life coaches, believing they were just "woo-woo" and not for someone as pragmatic as me. But my perception completely changed.

Then, there was my self-love guru (and tarot card reader), who would gently remind me to speak kindly to myself. Despite what skeptics may think, she provided oddly accurate and comforting insights.

But, the MVP of my healing squad was undoubtedly my therapist, Kelly. No matter how chaotic my thoughts were, she helped me untangle them, guiding me toward a greater understanding of myself.

Each of these incredible women, with their unique insights and advice, showed me ways to love myself better.

I was profoundly aware of my privilege, knowing not everyone could afford or access these professionals. But for me, the money spent wasn't an indulgence but an act of self-care. I was pouring resources into the most important project I could ever undertake – myself.

The Life Coach

The screen flickered on, and there was Melody.

"Hello," the life coach began, her voice warm and inviting.

"Hey," I replied, fidgeting nervously with the edge of my sleeve.

"How are you feeling today?" she asked.

I sighed heavily, "I'm frustrated about having to start over. It sucks."

Melody tilted her head, her eyes warm and attentive.

"Actually, you're not starting over," she replied.

My eyebrow arched upwards in a manner reminiscent of Dwayne 'The Rock' Johnson, reflecting my skepticism.

"You have thirty-six years of life experience behind you. You are not starting from scratch but from a place of wisdom and growth," she explained.

"I hadn't thought of it that way," I said.

"Your past experiences have shaped you into the person you are today. Now, you can use those lessons to navigate your way forward," she said.

Melody also reminded me that no experience was a total loss if I could extract a lesson from it.

"Write this down," she advised. "There are no failures - only wins and lessons."

This mantra shifted my perspective, allowing me to view failures not as negative experiences but as valuable learning opportunities.

Melody also encouraged me to face the 'mean girls' that were taking up way too much air time in my mind.

Was I expecting too much from Luke?
Was I the difficult one in the relationship?
Why was I so jealous?
Will I ever find love?
Am I even worthy of love?

"Ah, those thoughts can be tricky, can't they? But ask yourself, would you speak to a close friend the same way you're speaking to yourself now?" she asked.

I shook my head.

"I'd never say these things to people I love," I replied.

"When these thoughts pop into your head, ask yourself, 'Is this thought kind, true, or useful?' If it isn't, turn the channel."

Then, she proposed a fun idea to help me.

"Have you ever thought about giving these 'mean girls' names?"

I looked at her, puzzled, "Names?"

"Yes," she replied, a twinkle in her eye, "naming them makes them less intimidating. It helps you acknowledge their existence without giving them power over you."

And so, Harry and Carrie were born. With every session, I learned to tame them better. Whenever Harry or Carrie tried to whisper words of self-doubt into my thoughts, I'd retort, "Not today, Harry," or, "Quiet down, Carrie."

Note to Self:
Don't believe
everything
you think.

This playful approach allowed me to take control, making it easier to dismiss the pessimism that once held me back. It also created a degree of separation between myself and the harmful thoughts. I could recognize these thoughts as mere transient visitors in my mind rather than integral parts of my self-identity.

The Self-Love Guru

In the aftermath of my breakup, it became glaringly apparent that I needed more self-love in my life. The personal turbulence I had experienced was a clear sign that my inner world required attention and healing. I needed guidance to break the cycle of negative self-talk, which had become so deeply ingrained in me over time.

Enter Serena, my self-love guru.

"Close your eyes, take deep breaths, and let go of any external distractions," Serena instructed.

Under her gentle guidance, I would close my eyes and take deep, rhythmic breaths, releasing the stress and noise of the outside world.

However, it was after these soothing meditations that the real work began.

"Now, I want you to stand in front of the mirror and look into your own eyes," she said. "Say out loud, 'I am worthy. I am enough. I am loved.'"

And then came the kicker.

"I am a bad*ss," she said.

I nervously laughed. Was I really going to say that?

I took a deep breath.

"I am worthy. I am enough. I am loved," I paused. "And I'm a... bad*ss."

After the words left my mouth, I repeated them, but this time with more conviction.

"Hell, yeah, I'm a bad*ss," I said.

We both chuckled.

"See, it gets easier the more you do it," Serena advised.

She was right.

Additionally, Serena introduced me to techniques and exercises that helped me cultivate self-compassion between sessions.

"I want you to write three things you love about yourself every day. It's a powerful exercise in building self-love," she explained.

"What would you write today?" she inquired.

The prospect of stating out loud, even to a self-love guru, things that I loved about myself seemed unnatural, almost taboo.

"Um..." I stammered.

Serena patiently held my gaze, an encouraging smile gracing her lips.

"There's no rush. Take your time. It's okay," she said.

I took a deep breath in and then out.

"I... I love my resilience... my creativity," I continued, feeling a surge of courage. "And I love my laugh."

Naturally, in the face of this uncharted territory, I couldn't help but let out a laugh. Perhaps it was a defense mechanism or my way of processing this new exercise.

"Man, I really do love my laugh," I said.

"So do I," Serena noted.

These practices helped set a positive tone for the day ahead, allowing me to greet myself with kindness.

Near the end of each session, Serena would delicately draw a few cards from her well-worn Tarot deck. There was something magical about these beautifully illustrated cards.

She would ask me to focus on a question or a topic. Then, she would shuffle the deck with a meditative focus that I found intensely calming.

The soft rustling of the cards, the moment of anticipation as she drew them from the deck, and the final reveal held a ritualistic beauty that resonated deeply with me. She would then interpret the cards, weaving their meanings into narratives that strangely reflected my life at that time. (I know Tarot isn't for everyone; some might find it 'out there.' But it gave me hope and guidance.)

In one particularly memorable session, she drew the Lovers card, the Two of Cups, and the Queen of Cups in succession. With her fingers lightly touching the cards, her eyes sparkled with intrigue.

"I see a profound connection on the horizon," she said thoughtfully, her gaze alternating between me and the cards spread on the table.

"The Lovers card represents a deep, spiritual bond... and the Two of Cups signifies a mutual attraction and understanding. Finally, the Queen of Cups represents emotional openness and intuitive understanding. I see love coming into your life by fall."

I shook my head.

"I am planning on having a hot girl summer. I don't have time for love," I said.

She chuckled.

"That's fine. You can dismiss it for now. But the Queen of Cups is a reminder that you'll need to be open and receptive for this love to enter," Serena said.

I brushed it off, fully committed to enjoying the summer as a newly single woman. But Serena's words lingered in my mind, offering a glimmer of hope that when I was ready, love would be waiting for me again.

The Therapist

There's something transformative about sharing space with someone who listens to you, validates your experiences, and helps you navigate your way out of tangled emotional knots. That someone for me was Kelly, my therapist, who had been there as I processed my grandpa's death, quit my job, and then my breakup with Luke. She saw me blow up my life and stood by me. She was an anchor of stability.

One day, I found myself confronting a painful truth that I'd buried under layers of denial.

I stuttered, blinking back tears, "I feel...I feel so ashamed for staying in the relationship for as long as I did."

Kelly's voice, steady and compassionate, punctuated the silence. "Tell me more about that."

Swallowing the lump in my throat, I delved into what I'd been reflecting on.

"I think I stayed because I didn't want to disappoint people and also feared what other people might think of me. Marriage is celebrated as this incredible milestone in a woman's life, and I thought maybe the ring would make me happy and feel more secure in the relationship... but it didn't," I confessed.

"Our society has conditioned us to perceive the end of a relationship as a failure, as if it's a mark against our worth. But the truth is, every relationship we engage in is an opportunity for growth," Kelly said. "These societal constructs, like marriage, can often box us into making choices that may not align with our authentic selves. It's deeply ingrained in our culture. But remember, each of us has our unique path, and it doesn't have to look like anyone else's. Success is deeply personal, and so is happiness," she said.

"Yeah, but I still wonder what would have happened if I had communicated my needs better and upheld my boundaries earlier," I said.

Kelly nodded, acknowledging my introspection.

"It's important to remember that hindsight is 20/20. You made the best decisions you could with the information you had at the time. You can't beat yourself up about that. Give yourself grace and acknowledge your progress. You left the relationship. That takes bravery, so give yourself some credit," she reminded me.

I sat in silence, trying to absorb every word.

After a few beats, she added, "I hope it's okay for me to say this, but don't minimize the fact, Amber, that you were healing from two major surgeries and grieving your grandpa. And Luke, well, he was giving attention to someone else instead of you, his fiance."

I was sitting cross-legged on the floor of my childhood bedroom when Kelly's compassionate words washed over me like a much-needed hug. It was the sort of empathetic validation my younger self had once desperately sought and, even now, as an adult, deeply appreciated. It was not lost on me that the universe was seemingly orchestrating a return to where I started to help me understand where I needed to go.

And then, I did the most challenging thing of all: I forgave myself.

CHAPTER FOURTEEN

Becoming a Yinzer, N'at*

The month I spent residing with my parents was a priceless gift. Had I stayed in the bustling metropolis of New York City, this period of healing, filled with treasured memories, might have never transpired. However, the call to reclaim my independence became a necessity I couldn't ignore. It was time to find my own place and carve out a space that was mine.

Thankfully, my recent transition into a remote communications role opened the doors to a world of

---

*Here is a quick Pittsburghese translation guide:
Yinz = y'all
Yinzers = people who identify themselves with the city of Pittsburgh
n'at = and that
Ex. "Are yinz watching the Steelers, drinking I.C. Light, n'at?")

possibilities, offering me the luxury of geographic freedom and flexibility. I was free to go wherever my heart desired. While some may have dreamed of an exotic coastal locale or a picturesque European village, I had my eyes set on one city: Pittsburgh, Pennsylvania.

The Steel City had always held a unique allure for me. Some of my dearest friends from college had put down their roots there, so I'd visit the city once or twice a year. We'd grab an Iron City beer and a Primanti Brothers sandwich piled high with coleslaw and french fries at its OG location in the Strip District where I'd hope to spot Toni Haggerty, a local legend who has worked there since the 1970s. (Look her up!)

We'd also explore the city's beautiful parks and trails or catch a Steelers game at Heinz Field. (*By the way, I don't think I'll ever be able to call it Acrisure Stadium. #SorryNotSorry*)

Every visit left me smitten with its undeniable charm, so I decided to look into the practicalities of moving there.

My search began with exploring apartment listings in the city, assessing rent prices, locations, and amenities to determine if relocating there was a feasible next step for me. After scouring various websites, I stumbled upon a beautiful one-bedroom apartment with a breathtaking waterside view, lush green trees, a private pool, and a tranquil nature trail inches from my doorstep. A bonus? The apartment was a short drive from my parent's house, so I'd get to see them more. This apartment checked all the boxes (and then some), so I signed the lease. And just like that, a new chapter of my life began.

My parents once again assisted with my move, renting a U-Haul and filling it to the brim with my belongings to bring to my new home.

Note to Self:
It's never too late for a new beginning.

The moment I stepped into my new apartment, a wave of gratitude washed over me. I was glad to have my parents with me, their presence filling my new space with additional warmth and love. As the move-in day continued, the apartment gradually came alive with character. A flurry of activity – hammering, adjusting, positioning, and decorating. Each shelf we built, and every chair assembled felt like we were building not just furniture but my new life - piece by piece. When we stood back, we marveled at the beautiful sanctuary.

A celebration was in order, so my mom pulled out a bottle of wine. The sound of the cork popping was the closing note of our day; as she poured the deep crimson liquid into three glasses, a sense of satisfaction washed over us.

"To new beginnings," I toasted, raising my glass high.

"To new beginnings," my parents echoed.

Our glasses met with a satisfying clink; it was the perfect punctuation mark on an exhausting but rewarding day.

* * *

In the days that followed my move, my friends Caitlin and Dominique swung into action with their welcoming Pittsburgh spirit. Their enthusiasm for having me nearby was infectious, and they happily took on the role of my personal city guides. They invited me to events and local hangouts, where I could meet new people and make new friends. The warmth and generosity of everyone I met had a lasting impact, reminding me of the power of human connection.

I sought solace in the activities I'd always loved. I reveled in the euphoric atmosphere of live concerts. The beats from John Mayer and Machine Gun Kelly became the soundtrack to my summer, a therapeutic mix that allowed me to sing my heart out, shedding layers of past pain and wholeheartedly embracing the present.

I met fellow wine enthusiasts at the Pennsylvania Market and Wine Library, bonding over our shared passion for fine wine and great conversation.

At home, I basked in the warm summer sun, relaxing for countless hours by the pool. I also met neighbors who quickly became great friends, which rarely happens in NYC.

And as part of my self-care journey, I found the perfect manicurist, Michelle, who could elevate my nail game. From our first meeting, she exuded a warmth that immediately put me at ease. As she attentively cared for my nails, I recounted how I'd ended up in Pittsburgh, eventually divulging the details about my recent breakup and move.

"I pretty much blew up my life," I said.

"Well, congratulations!" she chimed.

Her voice bubbled with excitement as she rose energetically from her chair. I sat there, taken aback, as her response contrasted sharply with the usual waves of sympathy and pity I'd become accustomed to.

Without missing a beat, Michelle emerged with a basket overflowing with miniature bottles of alcohol, reminiscent of those served on domestic flights.

"Chardonnay... Pinot Noir... Cabernet..." she chanted, pulling out each mini bottle like a magician.

I took the Pinot.

She poured the wine into a glass and noted, "You're young, and you have a beautiful soul. You won't have trouble finding another guy—if that's even what you want."

Her reaction was a refreshing reminder that breaking free from a relationship can be a powerful act of self-love and self-care.

And, of course, one of the best advantages of my move to Pittsburgh was being a short drive away from my family. My nieces and nephew, especially, took delight in the proximity, making a special request well ahead of their tenth birthday— they longed to wake up in Pittsburgh on their big day, a wish I was more than happy to grant.

Quality time, my love language, became more than just a concept – it was now a reality. There were now spontaneous visits with my family, including more time with my grandma. The gift of time and closeness with them, unburdened by the constraints of distance and busy schedules, was truly priceless.

Pittsburgh did more than give me a new place to call home; it gave me the mental and emotional bandwidth to flourish and extend my boundaries. This expansion was mirrored perfectly in the growth of my @NotesToSelfShop Instagram page, which had evolved from a humble hobby to a thriving community of women bolstering each other through life's highs and lows.

In the year since I launched the social media page, women from around the world messaged me with comforting words like, "Your note was just what I needed today," or "Thank you for spreading so much positivity. I love your account."

Such feedback was incredibly humbling and deeply rewarding, reminding me these heartfelt messages were making a difference. So I decided to translate digital positivity into a business, creating notebooks, wall art, stickers, and journals.

It was awesome to see my content was making a difference in the lives of others worldwide, from the United States to Poland and the United Kingdom.

The Notes To Self Shop was off and running, offering a beacon of support, hope, and inspiration to anyone who needed it.

Note to Self:
Do what your
heart leads
you to do.

* * *

While I could wax poetic about my adoration for my new life in Pittsburgh, there were some skeptics. It's only natural that people were intrigued by my move to Pittsburgh, especially given my fifteen-year stint in the concrete jungle. Curious minds couldn't help but probe.

"Amber, don't you miss New York City?" a friend inquired. It was a valid question.

"I do find myself daydreaming about seeing new Broadway shows and still crave the taste of an everything bagel smothered in scallion cream cheese from Ess-a-Bagel in East Village, but truth be told, Pittsburgh is where I am meant to be right now," I replied.

Pittsburgh had its unique cultural flair, hosting touring Broadway shows every month, giving me plenty of opportunities to savor my passion for musicals. As for the bagel, I am still looking for a place that can replicate it. But thanks to the Internet, I can get these oversized bagels shipped right to my door.

"Wait, do you miss us?" the friend joked.

"Of course I do," I replied.

Each friend I made in New York left a mark on my life, from late-night conversations in dimly lit bars in Hell's Kitchen to impromptu dance parties in the bustling streets with the Empire State Building as our backdrop. We had navigated this wild city together.

At a Steeler's bar in the middle of Manhattan, I found an extraordinary group of friends, and we forged a close-knit community, cheering on the black and gold through victories and defeats. It wasn't just about football anymore but a shared sense of belonging.

I also had the incredible fortune of working with colleagues who became cherished friends. No matter where our journeys would take us, I knew these incredible people would always have a special place in my heart.

"Well, now I have an excuse to come back to New York all the time," I told the friend.

"So, like this weekend?" she jested.

* * *

Upon landing in NYC, a sea of men and women in crisp, carefully ironed uniforms, white, navy, and khaki, transformed the metropolis into a panorama of patriotic pride. It was officially Fleet Week, a time-honored tradition in the city, where the U.S. Navy, Marine Corps, and Coast Guard descend on the city.

My friends and I found ourselves in the company of service members and expressed our gratitude with several rounds of drinks.

I was sipping on a tropical concoction that tasted like sunshine in a glass, when a young Marine approached me. He resembled a *Titanic*–era Leonardo DiCaprio with a floppy mushroom cut and the most captivating smile. He was charming, funny, and attentive, and we shared stories about our lives, dreams, and aspirations. The alcohol undeniably facilitated our conversation and took a flirtatious turn when his hand subtly grazed mine, igniting a thrilling spark between us. Our lips came together, and it was as if the world paused in that brief, stolen moment. This was the first kiss

I'd shared with anyone since my breakup. And it felt good. As we pulled apart, we smiled at the moment's spontaneity.

"Can we do that again?" he cheekily asked.

We made out again (and again and again), each kiss more electrifying than the last; it was as if we were trying to capture every moment, etching it into our memories before he had to return to his ship. For me, the kiss was about simple, unattached joy, nothing more - affirming to myself that I was going to be just fine.

Our inevitable farewell arrived, and we sealed the evening with a final, lingering kiss. And with that, he drifted down the block, his figure slowly fading in the distance, never to be seen again. Sometimes people come into your life - only briefly - for a makeout session, and that's all you need.

The following day was a trip down memory lane as I checked out my old Hell's Kitchen stomping grounds. The neighborhood, while familiar, had new storefronts and refurbished facades that rendered it nearly unrecognizable to the grittiness I'd remembered. So much had changed that I nearly walked right by my old studio apartment.

The little mom-and-pop grocery store and my late-night pizza spot were gone. The buildings on either side of the apartment building were empty now, likely to be bought by some corporate business. The entrance to my apartment building was now a single black door with a fresh coat of paint. It made me suddenly miss the charm of the old, rusted one I'd entered so many times.

Standing on the corner of 48th Street and Ninth Avenue, a movie montage played in my head, showcasing all the unforgettable moments and memories I had created on this block. I could almost taste the oily delight of pizza slices devoured at 3 a.m. after a night out at Dalton's, a local sports bar where everybody knew my name.

And on this very block, I had shared kisses with many proverbial frogs. Each one taught me valuable lessons about love, life, and what I truly desired in a partner.

The glitz of my past life included unforgettable moments of my career, where I had the privilege of interviewing celebrities and rubbing elbows with some of the most influential people in the entertainment industry. Each memory was a time capsule. There was the evening I spent partying alongside Grammy-winning rapper Drake, where champagne flowed freely. Then, there was the private, invite-only concert featuring Mariah Carey, where I was close enough to see her delicately spritzed with her signature perfume, M by Mariah Carey, between each song.

I also had unforgettable face-to-face encounters with some of the GOATs (greatest of all time): Jennifer Aniston, Serena Williams, and Justin Timberlake. These exhilarating entertainment experiences, which most only dream about, resulted from my hard work and dedication.

My heart also fluttered at the recollection of the countless Broadway shows I'd been fortunate enough to see with their original casts, like Lin-Manuel Miranda in *Hamilton* and

Jonathan Groff, Lea Michele, and John Gallagher Jr. in *Spring Awakening*. These powerful performances transported me to other worlds and allowed me to escape the real world for a few hours.

But most importantly, my montage was filled with the warm, cherished memories of the fun nights spent with all my incredible friends. Our laughter, deep conversations, and shared experiences made my time in NYC unforgettable. As the reel of memories continued to play, I couldn't help but feel gratitude for the city that had given me so much.

Note to Self:
Only look back
to see how far
you've come.

New York would always hold a special place in my heart, but when my trip ended, I breathed a sigh of relief. The crowded streets and nonstop pace no longer appealed to me. I didn't miss it as much as I thought I would. Instead, I couldn't wait to get back to my new, quieter life.

Pittsburgh was now my home sweet home.

CHAPTER FIFTEEN

Puppy Love

After months of reveling in my independence, I discovered my life was about to turn upside down.

"Amber, your baby is here, and she is perfect!" I heard the voice on the other end of the phone say.

While most friends my age were sending their kids off to school, I was welcoming a new baby -- and by baby, I'm referring to an utterly adorable Italian greyhound puppy. She was about to fill my life with love, one adorable zoomie at a time. I named her Penny Lane as a nod to both my favorite movie *Almost Famous* and The Beatles.

My heart grew in ways I never imagined when I brought her home. Every tiny wag of her tail and playful scamper around the apartment amplified my happiness, making my home feel even more complete.

From day one, Penny was my little shadow, and I quickly learned that the term "personal space" didn't exist in her world. That tiny bundle of energy trailed me wherever I went, even to the most private quarters of my home, the bathroom. I was never alone with my thoughts again, and I didn't mind it at all.

She filled my days with laughter and snuggles, reminding me of the importance of both play and rest - a vital lesson often overlooked in the hectic world of adulthood.

Penny's playful and sweet presence was also a magnet for new people. Whenever we walked or visited the local dog park, her cute antics and loveable personality drew others in. I conversed with fellow dog owners and neighbors who couldn't resist her charm. I found myself sharing countless stories and adorable pictures with anyone who would listen. I even started her own Instagram page. (Yes, I was that dog mom.)

Seeing the world through Penny's innocent, trusting eyes helped me to realize that love, in its many forms, is something beautiful that we're all worthy of having.

* * *

Although I was pretty content with my life, I still felt an innate human desire for connection. I wondered if I could open my heart to the possibility of love again. So with a mix of curiosity and hope, I downloaded two popular dating apps, ready to explore the possibilities and make new connections.

An overwhelming wave of profiles greeted me. They were laden with gym selfies, featuring men showcasing chiseled physiques and confidently displaying their muscular biceps.

Swipe left.

Then there were the snapshots of men on fishing trips, proudly holding up their prized catches as if to say, "Look at what I can provide."

Swipe left.

After careful consideration, I swiped right on a few guys whose profiles showed promising potential. The first profile belonged to a man who proudly shared his expertise in winemaking. His description spoke of generations of family tradition, meticulously crafting his own vino with love and dedication, which immediately sparked my curiosity. I love wine, so wine not?

The second connection belonged to a man deeply immersed in politics. His profile description revealed his passion for making a positive impact on society. He conspicuously left out any mention of whether he identified as a Republican or a Democrat in his profile. It struck me as slightly peculiar, but then I pondered, perhaps it was inconsequential. After all, political leanings don't necessarily define a person or their potential as a partner.

When I finally embarked on those initial dates, I quickly realized that the chemistry I had hoped for failed to materialize in person, and conversations that had flowed effortlessly online now felt forced and awkward. It became apparent that the carefully curated personas on these dating profiles didn't align with reality.

"Wine guy" left me with the worst hangover of my thirties and ghosted me without a trace.

Meanwhile, the "Wannabe Politician" wanted to discuss every hot-button issue: abortion, guns, health care. I remained open to understanding his perspective. Still, when the topic changed to dogs -- and he voiced his disdain for these loving creatures -- I was done. Penny Lane and I were a package deal. Had he not looked at my profile?! Next!

Note to Self:
Life is too
short for
bad vibes.

I soon acknowledged that finding a genuine connection in a post-COVID world would demand more than just luck; I needed guidance to navigate this complex realm. I expanded my circle of support with someone who could help me navigate the complexities of modern dating.

In a serendipitous turn of events, I was introduced to Adelle, a certified love and relationship coach.

During our first meeting, the synergy between us was electric. Our conversations flowed seamlessly, punctuated by laughter, moments of reflection, and a mutual goal to help me navigate the dating world with more clarity.

After gaining insight into my past relationships, she immediately began updating my dating profile. She identified photos that didn't quite capture my true personality, replacing them with ones that genuinely showed off my passions and interests. Then, we collaborated on crafting a bio that struck a balance between lightheartedness and depth.

Adelle's insight also included invaluable tips on the types of profiles I should be swiping right on – those aligned with my values, aspirations, and relationship goals. Her advice centered around seeking genuine connections with individuals who shared my core values, encouraging me to prioritize emotional compatibility and shared interests over superficial attributes. As we collaborated on refining my Hinge profile, she asked why I hadn't considered using Bumble.

"Call me old fashioned, but I don't want to make the first move," I told her.

"Taking control of the conversation is empowering," she responded.

"I don't know. I'll think about it," I said.

That answer seemed to suffice for now, so we moved on to the next order of business: to write out my wants and needs in a future relationship. With a pen and a blank page, I jotted down my desires and non-negotiables for a future relationship.

Putting my intentions into writing made them feel tangible and achievable. I was opening the doors to the universe, inviting it to align the stars and bring me a partner who would genuinely love me, just as I am.

* * *

"Have you given any more thought to downloading Bumble?" Adelle inquired during our next meeting.

"Not really," I admitted, still uncertain about making the first move.

"Well, what do you have to lose?" she asked.

She had a point. So I downloaded the dating app, vowing that this time around, I'd be much more selective and not let myself go into endless swiping sessions. I didn't want to waste anyone's time, especially my own. I made a conscious effort not to let it consume my life.

I stayed anchored to my priorities, focusing on self-care and all the little things that brought me joy: friends, family, Penny Lane, theater, music, writing, river walks, wine tastings, and art. These were just a few of my favorite things. *(I really hope you sang that last line, à la Sound of Music.)*

Dear Universe,

While I am content alone, my heart is open to love, and I believe that the man I've been searching for is out there. I know that I deserve love, and I trust that you will bring him to me when the time is right.

I desire a man who is kind, has good morals, and demonstrates physical and emotional strength. He must be actively working on his personal growth or be in therapy.

He MUST love dogs.

I want a partner who treats me like a queen and communicates honestly about the direction of our relationship. He won't want to change me; he'll love me as I am -- not who I could be.

Communication, boundaries, financial stability, and authenticity are crucial to me.

I want someone who values family and can make me laugh (and yes, dad jokes count!)

While height is not a dealbreaker, a tall man would be a bonus. It would also be awesome if he can cook.

Above all, I seek someone who embraces me as I am, quirks and all.

With love,
Amber

Note to Self:
Don't forget to
fall in love with
yourself.

*   *   *

Mindlessly opening the dating app on my phone, I swiped through a few profiles when my gaze locked on Dallas, a tall, strikingly handsome man. As I read his profile, I couldn't help but notice the overlap in our interests: concerts, wine, and dancing. And most importantly, he loved dogs.

Swipe right.

Matched.

It was now on me to make the first move; it was a departure from the traditional dating dynamics I had encountered, where the ball was typically in the guy's court. But this time, I was excited to reach out.

Here goes nothing, I thought.

Dallas and I started exchanging messages on the app, and I quickly realized he was not only handsome but witty and charming. Our conversations flowed effortlessly, and he seemed genuinely interested in getting to know me. After a few days of messaging, he asked me out on a date; I was excited to see if our online chemistry would translate into the real world.

We had settled on a charming wine bar, and as I walked through the door, my heart fluttered with excitement. There he was – all 6'4" - just like his profile said. (It was a refreshing change from past experiences, where I had learned to take claimed heights with a grain of salt.)

Dallas greeted me with a warm smile and a gentle hug. Around us, the venue buzzed with conversation and the clinking of glasses, but it felt like it was just us for the next few hours.

Our conversation flowed effortlessly, punctuated by shared laughter and genuine curiosity about one another. It felt as if we had known each other for much longer than the brief span of our virtual courtship. There was a natural ease in our interaction. It felt so good.

"I'd like to do this again," Dallas said as we finished our drinks.

"Me, too," I replied.

I couldn't deny my attraction to him, but I was determined to approach love with a more grounded and realistic perspective. I consciously tried to stay present during our time together, genuinely enjoying his company. I was no longer focused on being the "cool girl" or how I could mold myself into the person I thought he wanted me to be.

As our relationship progressed, Dallas showed up for me in ways I hadn't experienced before. He bought me beautiful bouquets, something I specifically asked my exes to do, but they never did. With Dallas, I didn't even have to ask.

He helped me around my apartment, and we built furniture together without a fight ensuing. He kindly offered his support and assistance with a smile. It was refreshing. With Dallas, I was free to be my authentic self, which made me love him even more.

Better yet, he was not only there for me but also Penny. On the day of her spay surgery, I was a nervous wreck. Dallas could hear the anxiety in my voice, so he offered to come with me to the veterinarian's office so that we could pick up Penny together.

"It's going to be okay, babe," he said, putting his arm around me and hugging me tightly. His hug felt like home - safe and warm.

When the doctor bought Penny out, I was so happy to see my pup. She was still groggy, so Dallas scooped her up in his arms and cuddled her gently like she was his own. Even though my heart ached that she had to wear a cone, my heart melted as I watched Penny snuggle into him, trusting him completely.

"Thanks for being here for us," I told Dallas, my eyes filled with gratitude and happy tears.

"My pleasure," he smiled, his eyes exuding warmth.

Penny adored him, and that seemingly simple gesture spoke volumes about the kind of person Dallas was.

Together, our relationship wasn't a rollercoaster filled with ups and downs but rather a steady and secure partnership that was safe and fulfilling. It was a welcome change from the turbulent relationships I had experienced previously. With him, I discovered a profound truth: someone out there would not only respect my boundaries but also show up for me in ways I didn't know I needed.

Note to Self:
You were
always enough.

His calm and reassuring presence allowed me to let my guard down and fully be myself. I no longer had to spend countless hours wondering, "Is he into me?"

He understood the importance of being present and cherishing our shared quality time. He had a way of making me feel seen, valued, and loved. And I did the same for him.

I realized that our story could span eight months or fifty years, and both possibilities held their own beauty. I wasn't focused on timelines anymore -- only on my happiness.

I believe Dallas came into my life when I began showing up for myself with unwavering authenticity and stopped looking for someone else to complete me.

As I embraced my worth, set boundaries, and honored my needs and desires, I discovered a newfound sense of empowerment and self-respect. I was a complete and fulfilled individual, and Dallas became a delightful addition, like the whipped cream atop a delicious pumpkin pie.

In the aftermath of "blowing up my life," I found all types of love—the warmth of my partner's embrace, the fulfillment of a meaningful remote career, the unconditional love of Penny Lane, and the unbreakable bond between friends and family. Yet, amidst it all, I discovered the most extraordinary love story of all—the one I had with myself.

As the debris of people-pleasing and perfectionism cleared, I found myself standing amidst the beautiful ruins of who I used to be, and I saw, for the first time, the person I truly was meant to be.

No longer bound by the exhausting pursuit of others' approval or an unattainable ideal of perfectionism, I felt a liberating acceptance of my authentic self. I realized happiness was never about the job, the money, the city, or the relationship. Happiness was about embracing all of me with compassion and love. The recognition of my flaws and the acknowledgment of my scars (both mentally and physically) not only made me human but also served as profound badges of resilience and survival etched onto my being. I embraced my whole self - the good, the bad, the beautifully broken.

In the very act of blowing up my life, I found the freedom to be unapologetically me. Yes, I am still a work in progress, but I can confidently say that by leaving my comfort zone and following my heart, I found my way back home... to me.

CONCLUSION

My hope for this book is that it finds its way to someone who needs it. If you find yourself constantly overthinking and not taking action, or you know you need to walk away from something (a job, relationship, etc.) but are scared of ruining your life, I hope this book lights a fire in you. As I've shared candidly in my story, the decision to blow up my life didn't happen overnight. It took me hitting rock bottom to finally see I'd been settling for less than I deserved. I'm hoping my story helps you get to that conclusion sooner.

No one can tell you if you should "blow up your life." Only you can do that. But if you want to take the risk and make the leap, know you're not alone. You are stronger than you think and have the power to create a life aligned with your dreams and values. Now is the time to put your happiness first. (Remember, self-care isn't selfish.)

If you've been held back by fear, I want you to know that the potential rewards of taking risks - growth, discovery, fulfillment - outweigh the temporary discomfort and fear of venturing into the unknown. Don't just take my word for it. New research shows [1] that more people regret things they didn't do than what they did. This regret comes from knowing we didn't reach our full potential and lingering thoughts of "if we had only tried."

Take a moment to reflect on a part of your life that you've been yearning to transform, but the fear of taking that first step has been holding you back. Would you encourage a friend to stay in the circumstances you've been settling for? Do you want to end the year in the same place you started?

We can rationalize our inaction, convincing ourselves that we can't do, have, or achieve what we claim we so dearly want. But it all comes down to fear.

- **Fear of failure or rejection**

- **Fear of not being good enough**

- **Fear of the unknown**

- **Fear of conflict**

- **Fear of judgment**

- **Fear of change**

- **Fear of embarrassment**

- **Fear of not being perfect**

- **Fear of _____ (fill in the blank)**

But here's a truth bomb: fear is just an illusion. It's a story we tell ourselves, based on past experiences or future worries, with no basis in reality.

For the longest time, I thought I had to be perfect and feared failure. It kept me stuck. But today, I fully embrace life, knowing that even when things do not go as planned, it's an opportunity to learn and grow. I hope you will, too.

Don't forget that we are all human. Mistakes happen. Life throws us curveballs.

And so, we must give ourselves grace. And sometimes, in order to live life on your terms and in a way that feels so damn good to you, you have to blow up what's not serving you, like:

Negative self-talk
Limiting beliefs
Shame
Perfection
Comparisons
Doubts
Grudges
People's expectations
Toxic or draining relationships
False narratives

Letting go creates space for new and extraordinary blessings to come into your life. Releasing the wrong people or things, though sometimes painful and challenging, is one of the most important acts of self-love.

Don't ever settle, and be at peace, knowing you are worthy of love, success, happiness, and all of your wildest dreams exactly as you are today. It's not a question of 'when' you will become deserving but recognizing that you already are.

Remember, this is your journey, and you have the power to shape it into something extraordinary. Along the way, be kind to yourself, celebrate the wins, big and small, and let your light shine brightly for the world to see. You can achieve anything you set your mind to, so let this be the year you choose yourself and your happiness. You got this!

NOW, LET'S GO BLOW THIS SH*T UP!

ACKNOWLEDGMENTS

First and foremost, I would like to express my gratitude to you, beautiful reader, for purchasing my book and supporting my dreams. Because of you, I can share my stories, thoughts, and experiences with the world.

To Mom and Dad: Thank you for supporting my dreams of becoming a writer from the very beginning at the tender age of four. You embraced my creativity and inspired me to chase my wildest dreams. Your selflessness and love have allowed me to grow and flourish. I love you!

To Grandma: You and Grandpa taught me the importance of embracing life with enthusiasm, curiosity, and a zest for new experiences. I'll forever treasure our nights at the Little Theatre and our incredible weekends in NYC. Love you!

To Cara Alwill and Amanda Frances: I could not have brought this book to life without you both. You've been instrumental in my self-publishing journey, helping me see the importance of choosing myself rather than waiting to be chosen. Thank you!

To Adelle Kelleher: Thanks for making me download Bumble. <3

To Rebecca Babcock: Thank you for helping me through one of the most challenging times of my life. I am humbled and grateful for your support, empathy, and wisdom - and for always showing up for me, even as you went through your own health journey.

To Heather Tabacchi: With your keen eye and a little help from "Beyonce," you helped capture the essence of my story. Thank you for bringing my vision for this book cover to life.

To Molly: I am so grateful our paths came together. Thank you for your guidance, patience, and support. You have taught me valuable lessons about self-compassion and the importance of nurturing my mental and emotional well-being. From the bottom of my heart, thank you for your compassion and dedication to my healing journey.

To Jimmy, my Superman: You have swooped into my life and shown me true love, support, and partnership. Here's to many more chapters in our pretty dope love story.

To Dominque: We may not have been born sisters, but it feels like it. I hope you know just how much you mean to me. Thanks for reading every version of this book.

To Debbie: You show me every day that when women join forces, we can accomplish extraordinary things. Keep living the dream and being a ray of sunshine. (Please, give Joey and Chandler a big kiss for me.)

To JJ: Thank you for filling my life with infectious laughter and amusing stories. I'm grateful to call you my brother, and know I can always count on you when life gets hard.

To Kenneth, Morgan, and Alexus: As you grow and embark on your own journeys, always remember that the sky is the limit. Believe in yourselves, and never be afraid to explore, learn, and take risks. Dream big – and know I will be cheering you on every step of the way.

APPENDIX

Notes From Therapy

I am still a work in progress but wanted to share a few lessons from my therapy sessions – consider it a shortcut to self-improvement, no copay required. Some wisdom may resonate deeply with you, others might not, and that's okay. Everyone's journey is unique, so take what you need and leave the rest.

1. Make yourself and your mental health a priority. It is essential to prioritize your well-being and happiness above all else, ensuring that you care for yourself physically, mentally, and emotionally. Self-care is not selfish. By prioritizing yourself, you'll be better equipped to support and care for others.

2. Don't be afraid to set boundaries. Communicating boundaries is the foundation of any healthy relationship, whether it is with your partner, boss, or bestie. Most of the time, people are not trying to violate your limits—they just aren't aware of what they are. But by clearly defining your expectations, you communicate how you want to be treated. It is okay to hold people accountable if they disrespect your healthy boundaries. It might be time to reevaluate those relationships. Instead, surround yourself with individuals who respect boundaries.

3. Challenge negative thoughts. People-pleasing often stems from negative beliefs about oneself. Combat these thoughts when they arise and challenge their validity. Ask yourself if this thought is helpful or even true. Try replacing these thoughts with positive affirmations instead.

4. Use your voice. Finding your voice allows you to speak your truth. Embrace your individuality, share your thoughts and feelings, and stand up for what you believe in. Your voice is your superpower!

5. Be kind to yourself. Treat yourself with the same compassion and empathy you would extend to others, acknowledging your imperfections and mistakes without harsh judgment. Understand that you don't need to be perfect to be loved and accepted.

6. Find your cheerleaders. No one can do it all alone. Surround yourself with people who genuinely support and uplift you.

7. Know your worth, and don't settle. Embrace your value with unwavering confidence, understanding that you don't need to change or prove yourself to anyone, for you are already deserving of all the goodness life has to offer.

8. Harness the healing power of nature. Walking among the trees, beside a river, or simply breathing in the fresh air can work wonders for your mental health.

9. Forgive yourself for past mistakes. Acknowledge your past errors, learn from them, and then move on. Granting yourself forgiveness is a powerful act of self-compassion that opens the door to healing and personal growth.

10. Ask for what you deserve. Know that you can be thankful for the blessings in your life *AND* advocate for your needs and desires. You deserve happiness, fulfillment, and growth in all areas of your life.

RESOURCES

If you are looking for tools to help you on your journey of self-discovery, here are a few resources, including live online courses taught by the author.

Notes To Self: 30-Day Guided Journal

With daily prompts and exercises, this journal can help you uncover your values and priorities and develop a plan for achieving your dreams. Visit *NotesToSelfShop.com* to purchase your copy today.

Dare To Leap Masterclass

Do you find yourself scrolling endlessly on social media, feeling like everyone is living their best life, and you're still stuck? Do you know you need to walk away from things but are scared of ruining your life? If you said YES to any of these questions, I have the perfect program that will change your life. Dare to Leap is a four-week live masterclass designed for individuals who feel like they're being held back by the fear of making the wrong decision. Instead of continuing to dream about it, fantasizing about it, and thinking about it… you are going to be living it. Learn more at http://www. DareToLeapMasterclass.com.

Write Now or Never Course with Amber James:

D o you have a powerful story to share with the world? Do you want to self-publish a book that builds your business and inspires and helps others? Then join Write Now or Never, a live online course to learn how to self-publish your book, market it effectively, and leverage it to grow your business. Don't let fear or lack of knowledge keep you from sharing your unique message with the world. Join the waitlist and learn more at http://www.notestoselfshop.com/courses.

Seven Days to Get Out of Your Own Way

R eady to take action towards living the life you want? Download a free printable guided journal and start making progress today. This guide will help you overcome self-doubt and limiting beliefs and give you actionable steps to create the life you deserve. https://www.notestoselfshop.com/freebies/

ADDITIONAL RESOURCES

If you, or someone you know, is in emotional distress, in a crisis, or thinking about suicide, please call the National Suicide Prevention Lifeline number at 1-800-273-8255 (TALK), or call 211 or 911.

If you are in an abusive relationship, here are some resources that may help:

https://www.womenslaw.org/about-abuse/forms-abuse/emotional-abuse

https://www.freefrom.org/

I want to emphasize that I am not a licensed therapist or medical professional, and the information in this book should not be considered a substitute for professional advice. I have shared personal anecdotes with the intention of providing support to anyone who may be going through similar situations. I hope that by sharing my story, others can find comfort knowing they are not alone. Abusive relationships can leave us feeling isolated, confused, and doubting our sanity, but the emotions you are going through are valid, and there is hope for healing and a brighter future.

It is important to consult with qualified therapists, counselors, or medical professionals who are experts on narcissism or abuse for personalized guidance and support. If you are experiencing relationship issues, or any form of abuse, I strongly encourage you to seek help from trusted professionals who can provide appropriate assistance to help you navigate your unique situation.

CITATIONS

[1] Gilovich, T., & Medvec, V. H. (1994). The temporal pattern to the experience of regret. *Journal of Personality and Social Psychology, 67*(3), 357–365. https://doi.org/10.1037/0022-3514.67.3.357

ABOUT THE AUTHOR

Amber James is an author, speaker, and former red-carpet reporter. Her work has been featured prominently in CNN, MTV, and *Us Weekly*. Now, she channels her storytelling prowess into empowering women globally with her wildly popular Instagram @NotesToSelfShop and corresponding 30-day journal, *Notes to Self*. She currently resides in Pittsburgh with her dog, Penny Lane.

Connect with Amber
http://www.notestoselfshop.com
Instagram: @NotesToSelfShop
amber@notestoselfshop.com